95

THESES FOR
THE CHURCH

BEN JOHNSON

PRESS

©1995 CTS Press

ISBN 1-885121-14-8
Design by Melissa Mahoney

CTS Press
P.O. Box 520
Decatur, GA 30031

PREFACE

This book represents a new challenge for mainline denominations, largely because the world has changed. More and more persons fall into the category of "unchurched" and this growing conglomeration of secular persons has a special character. As a result, the church's old techniques will no longer work.

Still, many mainline congregations continue as though nothing has changed since the Eisenhower presidency. Tragically, their declining numbers tell the tale of a church out-of-touch with the rapidly changing world it surrounds.

These *95 Theses for the Church* constitute an attempt to awaken denominations and theological seminaries to their plights. They have been written for pastors, church leaders, and seminarians.

These theses do not presume to offer a complete diagram of the church situation. Instead, each one provides an invitation to conversation, reflection, and evaluation. I hope these sometimes terse statements will serve the conversation, eliciting concern and interest, precipitating healthy change in congregations who are seeking direction.

Perhaps using the term "95 Theses" is a bit presumptuous. I hope it will not seem so. I hope instead it will be seen as an effort to call attention to the crisis of today just as Martin Luther's original theses, hammered with conviction to the Wittenburg door, called attention to the issues of the 16th century.

I look forward to your responses as we consider together the kinds of changes that serious dialogue can bring about.

BEN JOHNSON
June 1, 1995

FOREWORD

Ben Johnson is among those who have thought long, well, and hard about the future of the church. Along with his wide range of conversation partners, Johnson faces the deep cultural crisis in which we live, and the church's tricky, complex relation to that cultural crisis. In my perception, Johnson's work revolves around three intimately linked accents.

First, Johnson has worked for a very long time on issues of evangelism, by which he surely means the old-fashioned enterprise of "bringing persons to Christ" in a way that results in church growth. Second, more recently, he has recognized that a deep emptiness among those already in the church – pastors included – requires a move "beyond evangelicalism" to issues of spirituality, by which he evidently means attentiveness to communion with the living God. But third, Johnson guards against a spirituality that is excessively privatistic. And so he stresses structural, institutional dimensions of the crisis facing the church. In asking questions about public issues and matters of polity, Johnson joins in the growing awareness that there is no easy "fix" to the life of conventional "mainline" Christianity.

These three accents – evangelism, spirituality, and ecclesial awareness – lie behind this offer of theses. It is of course no accident that Johnson's theses number ninety-five, a direct and intentional allusion to the frontal challenge of Martin Luther. Johnson has no personal ambition to replicate the role of Luther. But he does recognize that this moment in the Western church (including the U.S. church) is not unlike Luther's urgent moment, in that the issues are acute, the risks are very great, and the gospel opportunities are enormously open. Johnson offers "theses," a mode peculiarly appropriate to his own style of faith and life. The genre of thesis insists that the statement be taken with great seriousness and argued through, not flinching from disagreement that is serious, well-spirited, and informed. At the same time, Johnson understands and intends that the theses are not fixed conclusions, but are probes which require, permit, and may legitimate new thinking. Johnson knows full well that old formulations – liberal or conservative – cannot be relied upon in the face of a crisis that is very broad but also elemental.

In the end, what is clear from Johnson's offer is that he is through and through a practical theologian. That is, he invites reflection that is pertinent to what is "on the ground" in the church. And he knows full well that what is now required is not yet more speculative theory, but lived efforts to receive new modes of church life, faith, and witness.

Ben Johnson is not a simple man. There is richness, depth, and complexity to his thought and his urging. All of that richness, however, is rooted in a simplicity of faith from which emerges his daring thought. What will reward Johnson for the risks he takes here is not facile agreement, but a serious engagement whereby we move in shared reflection to a faith that none of us alone can imagine or embrace. I am grateful to Ben for his effort, and count him as a friend and colleague, as we seek a "better city."

WALTER BRUEGGEMANN
Columbia Theological Seminary
November 30, 1994

95 Theses for Today

Thesis #1
"To manifest the Presence of God in our time the church must respond to its changed context."

Thesis # 2
"The church today stands at the end of an era: a new day lies before the church."

Thesis #3
"The church ministers in a rapidly changing culture and if the church does not adapt its message, strategy, and structure to these changes it will fail in its mission."

Thesis # 4
"The church seeks to carry out its mission in a 'post-Christian' world wherein the presuppositions that have supported the Christian world view, values, and style of life no longer dominate the U.S. culture."

Thesis #5
"The society in which the church ministers is 'post-Constantinian,' which suggests that the church has no favored position with the government and the social structures."

Thesis #6
"The world in which ministry takes place is also 'post-modern': the world of the Enlightenment has collapsed and a new vision that offers coherence and meaning has not yet come into being."

Thesis #7
"The ministry of the church must take place in a post-denominational world in which old loyalties and distinctions have been seriously eroded."

Thesis #8
"The culture in which the church ministers has become increasingly secular, meaning that most persons believe they can manage life, politics, and morals without reference to God."

Thesis #9

"The culture is also pluralistic with every competing view of life and the world standing on equal footing; each view is considered equally good and no one has the right to question the view of another."

Thesis #10

"Because the electronic media has become the dominant mode of communication the church must discover how to minister to a visual culture."

Thesis #11

"Mainline churches have been disestablished in the prevailing culture and continue to decline in numbers and influence."

Thesis #12

"Congregations today have their ministry in a missionary situation without the previous supports to which they had become accustomed."

Thesis #13

"Most congregations remain totally unprepared to cope with the changed situation and as a consequence continue to decline."

Thesis #14

"A disproportionate number of congregations face discouragement from their failure of mission and dissension arises between church leaders and pastors."

Thesis #15

"Mainline denominations are experiencing the judgment of God intended for our correction and redirection."

Thesis #16

"Most congregations are in dire need of transformation and revitalization which includes:
A Recovery of a Sense of the Presence of God,
A Shift from 'Maintenance' to Mission,
The Revitalization of Worship,
The Liberation of the Laity,
The Selection and Nurturing of Mentors,
The Formation of Small, Intentional Groups."

Thesis #17
"Mainline churches need to recover a sense of the Presence of God in their life and ministry."

Thesis #18
"We need to recover the conviction that church is about God and a people – a people who love, worship, and obey God."

Thesis #19
"When the church prays, it postures itself to hear what the Lord of the church will say."

Thesis #20
"We need to repent with the assurance that God chooses to be revealed to the congregation that turns from its own way to the way of God."

Thesis #21
"The rebirth of the church occurs through encounters with God and the world God has created."

Thesis #22
"Women are bringing a renewed sense of the Spirit and a model for authentic spirituality to congregations."

Thesis #23
"The churches of the mainline must shift from a maintenance mentality to a missional passion."

Thesis #24
"Most congregations revere the past more than they anticipate the future."

Thesis #25
"A past orientation leads to the repetition of old programs and practices that do not take into account the changed context."

Thesis #26
"Repetition of old forms leads to veneration and finally to the sacralization of form without substance."

Thesis #27

"The tradition of too many churches is sacrosanct and therefore is defended and preserved at all costs."

Thesis #28

"Because of the veneration of the past many congregations resist any change in form, vision, and mission."

Thesis #29

"Congregations that refuse to change are destined to die and further fuel the decline of mainline churches."

Thesis #30

"To foster new life, stagnant congregations must embrace the reality of their present context and imagine their life in new forms."

Thesis #31

"The transformation required will be life-giving to some but will seem like death to others."

Thesis #32

"Women have proved adept at revitalizing ineffective, declining, and often hopeless congregations."

Thesis #33

"All effective pastors (male and female) are destined to become more effective practical theologians who equip congregations to discern their mission in a changing world."

Thesis #34

"One key to the shift from maintenance to mission will be the change in orientation from program to persons."

Thesis #35

"The biblical injunction 'to make disciples' offers the most logical starting point for this reorientation of mission."

Thesis #36

"The average congregation needs a revitalization of worship."

Thesis #37

"The time, place, and manner of worship must be opened to critique in light of the kinds of persons to whom the church offers ministry."

Thesis #38

"The form of worship needs to be more accessible to those who have not been shaped by the tradition of a particular church."

Thesis #39

"The language of worship requires words, gestures, and sounds that are understood by the participants."

Thesis #40

"The service of worship should aim to incarnate the Presence of God in the culture and life of the worshipping people."

Thesis #41

"Music of praise to God can have variety, relevance, and contemporary appeal without losing its integrity."

Thesis #42

"Whatever the language, style, or form, the service of worship aims to enable persons to encounter the presence of the Living God in praise, confession, and obedience."

Thesis #43

"Altering the worship of a congregation will prove to be the most challenging and the most risky change it faces."

Thesis #44

"The Laity – People of God – in Future Church will be liberated for ministry both in the church and in the world."

Thesis #45

"Every baptized person has a vocation in and through Jesus Christ."

Thesis #46

"Each person possesses particular gifts for ministry."

Thesis #47

"All baptized persons need support and guidance to claim and use their gifts for ministry in the church and in the world."

Thesis #48

"There is no qualitative distinction between ministry in the church and ministry in the marketplace."

THESIS #49

"A primary task of the ordained minister is the equipping of the baptized for ministry."

THESIS #50

"The laity in Future Church will claim their voice in the governance of the church."

THESIS #51

"The church must be intentional about developing spiritual mentors who model, nurture, and pass on the faith to children and secular seekers."

THESIS #52

"Most congregations tend to reproduce themselves in the form of cultural Christians, blurring the distinction between prevailing cultural norms and the Christian lifestyle."

THESIS #53

"As the new millennium dawns, leaders of congregations need to define what it means to be 'Christian' in a secular age and formulate plans for developing mentors of 'apostolic' Christianity."

THESIS #54

"To fulfill this task the church must issue the call and provide the training to equip effective spiritual mentors."

THESIS #55

"One responsibility of a mentor will be to assume oversight of the People of God."

THESIS #56

"In the twenty-first century the evangelistic task of the church will be accomplished in part through spiritual mentors. (Christianity has always been better caught than taught!)"

THESIS #57

"The best way to initiate the needed transformations in the church will be through the formation of small, intentional groups – cadres of apostolic believers!"

Thesis #58

"The re-formation of the whole begins with the transformation of the few – persons who are salt, light, and leaven."

Thesis #59

"Persons called to this adventure must agree to meet together regularly for an agreed upon length of time in an agreed upon place."

Thesis #60

"The small community will begin with simple disciplines that constitute the community of Christ."

Thesis #61

"This disciplined group will intentionally reach out to others and include them in its communal life."

Thesis #62

"This intentional community will provide the setting for personal transformation, leadership development, and equipping for mission and ministry."

Thesis #63

"The future of the church depends upon leaders who have been birthed, formed, and nurtured in the environment of vital faith."

Thesis #64

"The selection, training, and support of the leaders for these small, intentional communities will be a primary task of ordained ministers."

Thesis #65

"The spiritual life and vision of a community of lay ministers provides vital respite, nurture, and support for weary pastors."

Thesis #66

"Because of today's radical and abrupt cultural changes, clergy face dislocation and ever increasing stress."

Thesis #67

"Most clergy have been prepared to pastor congregations that no longer exist."

Thesis #68

"Contextual changes have been so swift and pervasive that clergy have been unable to make the necessary adjustments."

Thesis #69

"Old models of ministry are inadequate for the present age."

Thesis #70

"Clergy will probably find their greatest source of help in pondering the role and image of the minister of God set forth in the Old and New Testaments."

Thesis #71

"An effective model of ministry flows out of and is accompanied by the minister's embrace of a serious spiritual journey."

Thesis #72

"As they journey with God, clergy will learn anew to speak of God in simple, personal, and experiential terms."

Thesis #73

"Effective clergy will claim their authority without becoming authoritarian."

Thesis #74

"Secure pastors will liberate, welcome, equip, and support the lay apostolate."

Thesis #75

"Ministers of God must resist the temptation to alleviate their stress through immoral sexual liaisons, drugs, alcohol, or the consumption of goods and pleasure."

Thesis #76

"Above all, clergy who are pioneering a new day for the church will not retreat from the struggle to equip the new church to meet the challenges forced upon it."

Thesis #77

"Women and men have an equal partnership in the transformation of the ministry of Christ."

Thesis #78

"The relevant seminary will radically alter its vision, curriculum, and priorities to prepare ministers for their tasks in the emerging world."

Thesis #79

"The forward-looking seminary will shift from a maintenance to a missional program of training, recognizing that it is equipping missionaries to work in a culture alien to the gospel."

Thesis #80

"Both seminary curriculum and the style of teaching should be informed by the shifts in the culture and the gifts candidates bring to their training."

Thesis #81

"Seminaries should be as committed to excellence in spiritual formation for future ministers as they are to excellence in academic preparation."

Thesis #82

"The seminary community should conduct its life in a manner that models Future Church."

Thesis #83

"Seminaries will be called to fill a new role as a result of the demise of national denominational bureaucracies."

Thesis #84

"Theological seminaries will fulfill their mission only as they become servants of the church and respond to new demands placed upon them."

Thesis #85

"Any seminary curriculum that does not aim at preparing ministers for effective ministry in a changed church in a changing world is irrelevant."

Thesis #86

"Teachers and leaders in the seminary are called to confess their sins as participants in the creation and support of Future Church."

Thesis #87
"Mainline churches as we have known them for the past century are in disarray and decline, facing death."

Thesis #88
"The loss of members, the loss of influence, the loss of established place in the society, and the unwillingness to face the reasons for these losses herald our demise."

Thesis #89
"A disproportionate number of congregations are in conflict with themselves, their ministers, and the national church."

Thesis #90
"The national church has falsely envisioned itself as the true and faithful church hampered by the lagging vision of congregations."

Thesis #91
"The national church has for the most part lost touch with the 'grass roots.'"

Thesis #92
"The national church has lost credibility with many pastors, local congregations, and judicatories."

Thesis #93
"The national church will continue to experience diminishing funds."

Thesis #94
"The future mainline denomination cannot be birthed by the present bureaucratic leadership."

Thesis #95
"New and living congregations with visionary pastors will give birth to new structures and appropriate judicatories for the church of the future."

CONTEXTUAL
PERSPECTIVE

THESIS #1
To manifest the Presence of God in our time the church must respond to its changed context.

For the church to be effective it must thoughtfully and prayerfully respond to the time and place in which it exists. "Contextualization" means that the church takes root in a particular place, expressing its ministry to and through persons shaped by a particular culture. While contextualization proves vital to communicating the gospel, it also presents a dilemma since culture not only shapes those whom the church seeks to reach but also the church itself. The church often bears the marks of culture unconsciously. Yet, as culture changes in aim and substance, the church must consciously adapt its vision and methods while remaining faithful to God's revelation in Jesus Christ.

Of course, while seeking to relate to the culture, the church must always resist any temptation to be co-opted by culture. Former missionary Lesslie Newbigin saw fellow missionaries in India affirming the oppressive caste system in order to avoid offending the people they sought to evangelize. The gospel, says Newbigin, must be communicated in the language and symbols of those to whom it is addressed, but "how far should the gospel be 'at home' in a culture, and how far should it resist domestication?"[1]

That question arises in every Christian community on every continent - but it seems especially significant in the United States, where the context for ministry has changed radically in the last 50 years. For example, an electronic, visual culture creates a different context from a print culture; the capacity to travel creates an interface of cultures that just a few decades ago rarely interacted. These kinds of changes force the church to rethink how it "incarnates," or embodies, its life and witness in a particular culture.

Such a contextualization occurred in the flesh-and-blood experience of Jesus of Nazareth, from whom the church receives its foundation and direction for ministry. The birth stories about Jesus indicate that the Spirit of God acted in concert with a young woman to create divine life in her womb. God was manifested in the humanity of Jesus.

The goal of incarnation has been the intention of God from the dawn of creation. First, in a nation (Israel), then in a person (Jesus Christ), and ultimately in humanity (Kingdom of God). The church represents Jesus Christ in and to the world. As has been said, While Christ's first body was born in Bethlehem and named Jesus, Christ's second "body was born at Pentecost in Jerusalem and was called the 'church.'"[2]

THESIS # 2
The church today stands at the end of an era: a new day lies before the church.

The church in North America faces the close of an era which offered a favored position in the culture.

Since the founding of America, the Christian church has been viewed as the nation's moral conscience. It has provided leaders for crucial roles in government, education, and the arts.

Although the church in the United States has never been funded by or governed by the state, it has received favored treatment, creating an informal alliance between church and state. The church received further legitimization and implicit power through its members who served in government legislatures and state houses. This implicit establishment has eroded.

The church's disestablishment has taken place at three important junctures in America's history. The first occurred when the federal Constitution and Bill of Rights severed the official bond between church and state inherited from Roman Emperor Constantine and the marriage of church and state in Western Europe 15 centuries before. The second occurred with a change in the national mood. After World War I, inflation, unemployment, racial tensions, and political partisanship led to a growing disillusionment which "undermined the attraction to mainstream Protestantism's crusading spirit." Third, the turmoil of the 1960s brought a cultural disestablishment to mainstream Protestantism. The questioning of authority challenged the church's right to take any role in shaping culture.[3]

As a consequence of these changes the church must learn how to be faithful to God in a culture that does not afford it favored status. The shift from favored status to "marginal" status may provide the challenge that "mainline" churches need to rethink their role and mission. Serious rethinking of the church's life drives us to examine the dynamic life of the first century church that had neither favored status nor a safe place in the nation.

The new day before the church could be a rebirth of "apostolic Christianity" in which the energy of the Spirit pushes the church in new directions with great effectiveness (Acts 1:8). If the denominations reject this call to "newness," we are likely to see further erosion of membership, financial support, and effective mission.

THESIS #3

The church ministers in a rapidly changing culture and if the church does not adapt its message, strategy, and structure to these changes it will fail in its mission.

By nature cultures remain in the process of change. But consider the pace of cultural change in North America over the past 50 years. The technological revolution has made instant communication possible. The growing "information superhighway" allows people to access, handle, and store vast amounts of information without ever leaving the home or office. Increased mobility enables persons to visit several nations in the space of a week. The collapse of the Soviet Union has challenged the 'cold war' myth perpetuated for half a century in our nation. These and a host of lesser influences have created a different audience for the message of the gospel.

The church must communicate the good news of Jesus Christ in such a manner that the minds and values shaped by this changing culture can hear it. Adapting the message does not mean sacrificing the essential truth of the gospel – in Jesus Christ the world is reconciled to God. Yet what language, metaphors, and experiences of the faith can make the gospel real for this generation?

For example, how can a church that promotes self-denial attract Baby Boomers committed to self-fulfillment? "The fact is that the more strongly one holds to an ethic of self-fulfillment, the less likely one is to belong to the church."[4]

The changes in our context call for rethinking our mission strategy. For decades we have embraced a top-down approach as local congregations submitted to programs passed down by national headquarters. The new era will not be so shaped and guided.

Local congregations have unwisely been structured so that persons are enlisted to do tasks they did not conceive and to carry out plans they had no part in making. Many structures have been cumbersome and slow to react to changes. Programs have been conducted out of loyalty to the past, not in response to a specific need. Perhaps the management model of ministry has served its purpose and we need a deeply personal, Spirit - inspired structure more sensitive to persons.

THESIS # 4

The church seeks to carry out its mission in a "post-Christian" world wherein the presuppositions that have supported the Christian world view, values, and style of life no longer dominate the U.S. culture.

The term "post-Christian" describes the church's situation in contemporary culture. The idea of Christendom, or the Christian world, has roots in the thousand year period between about 500 and 1500 A.D. when most of life in the Western world was organized and nourished by the church.

For example, the intellectual life of the community was shaped by the basic tenets of the Christian faith. Writings that did not support the faith were banned by the church. The political life of the empire or nation had close ties with the Pope and the college of bishops so that kings and emperors were subservient to the biddings of religious leaders. Art, literature, and music had religious themes; and, theater productions were often commissioned by the church. The church's pervasive involvement in every aspect of life sacralized it.

It would be unthinkable to be born into that culture and not be baptized, believe in God, or attend the church. But some were not baptized due to a lack of priests. Yet where the church was present, the atmosphere of faith was pervasive. The local cathedral served not only as the place where people worshiped God but also as the school, the theater, and even the local motel for travelers.

This cultural structure was the product of "Christendom," a period when all of life was organized around the church and in accordance with values dictated by the church hierarchy. The church established itself as the distributor of grace and eternal life. To disobey the teaching of the church met with serious reprisals including excommunication from the church and from eternal life.

This synthesis of religion and culture, faith and life, that we call Christendom broke apart under the impact of two powerful forces. First, Martin Luther in the Protestant Reformation questioned the absolute authority of the church. Second, Rationalist thinkers of the 17th and

18th centuries took his original protest to its logical end, shattering the church/world synthesis. Luther shifted the norm from the authoritative church to the authoritative Word, and Enlightenment thinkers shifted the locus of authority from the Word of God to human reason.

In the 250 years since the dawn of the Enlightenment, radical shifts have taken place in Western culture, with the church being largely driven from the public arena. Today only 28 percent of Americans consider the church relevant to the way they live today.[5]

During Christendom, the word "Christian" carried vastly different connotations from the meaning coined in Antioch (Acts 11:19-26), where a "Christian" strictly followed Christ and protested prevailing political currents.

The modern church cannot rely on approval or support from the public sector. In fact, when the church speaks it can now expect to meet with hostility because the culture believes the church has no right to act in the public sphere. Increasingly the church has been consigned to personal values and ecclesiastical rituals.

Today, the meaning of "Christian" more closely parallels original New Testament connotations. We are no longer privileged. Yet we may find, as New Testament Christians did, that marginalization fosters a healthy church.

THESIS #5
The society in which the church ministers is "post-Constantinian,"
which suggests that the church has no favored position with the
government and the social structures.

The terms "post-Constantinian" and "post-Christian" have a kinship. Christendom began when the Roman Emperor Constantine legitimized Christianity as the religion of the empire through his Edict of Milan in 313 A.D. This marked the fusion of the concerns of the church and the empire.

Someone has said that with respect to religion, the Roman citizens believed all religions to be equally true; the Roman philosophers believed all religions equally false; and the Emperors believed all religions were equally useful. Christianity did become a "useful" tool for maintaining control and promoting cohesion.

Loren Mead suggests that the edict of Milan made the faith not only acceptable but compulsory. In the apostolic days the church knew where the mission began – "outside the door." When worship ended the mission began because the small community of believers lived among pagans. With the empire's adoption of the faith, everyone was baptized and "overnight" the empire became Christian. Suddenly the mission field no longer existed at the front door of the church but at the frontier of the empire. The role of members shifted radically from being missionaries to supporting missionaries.

The role of a lay person after the Edict of Milan was to support the church financially, live a moral life in accord with the church's teaching, and to be a good citizen of the empire. This shift in mission transformed vital, active missionaries into passive observers and obedient servants.

When, therefore, we say that the church has its ministry in a post-Constantinian era, we are pointing to the church itself, the context of mission, and the missionaries. The Constantinian church brought persons into the church by the scores, but these persons lacked the careful instruction and nurture provided during the first few centuries. These nominal believers (if that) not only did not know the faith but often were made Christian at the point of the sword. Membership in the church was mandated and thus shallow. Constantine created a church of nominal Christians.

With mission moving to the frontier of the empire, Christians became passive in their missionary activity. It was as though the only task of the church was to hold to its massive gains at the center and expand on the periphery.

To be in a post-Constantinian situation in ministry requires us to look first at the character of membership within the church. We can no longer afford passive observers ignorant of the faith and careless in their lifestyle. If we are to bear witness to our neighbor, our lives must in some sense be different from theirs.

Second, we must recognize that the mission field is no longer "out there somewhere." Individualism is one of the few remaining orthodoxies of American culture writes Robert N. Bellah.[6] It is now common for individuals to construct their own religion from available ideas, supermarket fashion. Clearly, in a post-Constantinian church the field for mission moves back to the door of the church.

THESIS #6

The world in which ministry takes place is also "post-modern":
the world of the Enlightenment has collapsed and a new vision that
offers coherence and meaning has not yet come into being.

By "post-modern" I am referring to the era when the rational proposals of the Enlightenment have disintegrated. The Enlightenment thinkers rejected both the church and the scriptures as their source of authority, substituting human reason in place of these authorities.

With this break from the church, the philosophers of the Enlightenment affirmed only one valid source of knowledge – sense perception. True and certain knowledge, they said, comes through the senses. This way of knowing gave birth to the scientific method of observation, hypothesis formation, and testing or experimentation.

Much of that narrowness persists in today's thinking, writes Parker Palmer. "There is an illness in our culture; it arises from our rigid separation of the visible world from the powers that undergird and animate it. With that separation we diminish life, capping off its sources of healing, hope, and wholeness."[7]

Of course, the scientific method has provided numerous insights and new technologies. Many of these discoveries have been instrumental in saving human life and making life better for large groups of persons. For all these life-enriching creations we can only be grateful.

Yet, philosophers of the Enlightenment claimed that human reason could create a common morality. Since the morality of the church was rejected as antiquated and authoritarian, nothing but reason remained to fill in this gap.

Philosophers of the Enlightenment failed only to question purpose. Granted the scientific method led to many new discoveries, granted that knowledge multiplied repeatedly. But, for what purpose would this new accumulation of knowledge be used? "If I do not know the purpose for which human life was designed, I have no basis for saying that any kind of human life-style is good or bad. It is simply an example of human life as it is." Unfortunately the leaders of the Enlightenment assumed that "knowledge was good in and of itself" and that progress toward the betterment of life would be inevitable.

The facts seem to repudiate many of these Enlightenment assumptions. The confusion about sexual norms reveals the inadequacy of human reason to solve ethical questions. The instruments of war and mass destruction deny that progress is inevitable. If these do not disprove

Enlightenment optimism, then certainly Hiroshima and Auschwitz do. Ministry today takes place in a context of moral confusion in which many people question the power of science, reason, or even faith to address human problems. Christian thinkers must find the creativity to imagine a new world.

THESIS #7
The ministry of the church must take place in a post-denominational world in which old loyalties and distinctions have been seriously eroded.

This loss of denominational loyalty in North American culture has particular significance for the growth and outreach of the church. In past generations the church assumed that if members had children, baptized them, and taught them the faith that these children would naturally be loyal to the church.

Such loyalty is becoming increasingly rare among younger generations. Americans raised during the Depression are known for brand loyalty - from the cars they buy to the denominations they attend. Baby Boomers tend to value personal fulfillment over loyalty. This attitude "...means a willingness to switch to another church if [one's] needs will be met there."

A strange shift has taken place in American religious life – denominations have become interchangeable. A person baptized Methodist might as readily join a Lutheran or Presbyterian congregation if that congregation seems to meet his or her needs.

Three things have inadvertently contributed to this loss of denominational loyalty: the ecumenical movement, the automobile, and the shopping mentality. Denominations, in an effort to fulfill the will of Christ that "they all may be one" (John 17:21) joined in a council of churches to seek unity. Due to a desire for unity and for economic frugality, common curricula were developed and the broader and more inclusive the base, the greater loss of denominational distinctiveness. Such curriculum produced a "faith in general" without corresponding loyalty to a particular denomination.

The automobile has undermined the parish mentality by affording persons the ability to go to whatever church they choose. In decades past it was necessary to attend a church within driving distance of the horse and buggy or within walking distance of one's home. Under these circumstances persons went to churches based on their geography. But with the advent of the automobile these restraints were swept away because mobility made it possible to attend a church 30 or 40 miles from home. In *Dying for Change*, Leith Anderson points out that "While mobility is mostly a matter of physical relocation, it is also a mentality. Just as we may move from city to city or house to house, we may also move from marriage to marriage, ...job to job [or church to church]."[8]

The influence of advertising and shopping centers has created a "shoppers' mentality" for most Americans. This mindset is determined not by the denomination of birth but preference. So just as one shops for a new pair of shoes or a new car, people shop for a church. Instead of maintaining old loyalties, many persons decide which church to attend in the same fashion as they buy shoes or automobiles – what "pleases me." What meets my need. What fulfills my expectations.

To increase attendance and to grow as a church, a local congregation cannot depend upon denominational loyalty. The loss of denominational distinctions, on the other hand, may give birth to a livelier church than we have known to this point.

THESIS #8
The culture in which the church ministers has become increasingly secular, meaning that most persons believe they can manage life, politics, and morals without reference to God.

A secular society stems from the breakdown of Christendom. Because Christian faith is neither embraced nor legitimated by the state, the language and activities of faith have been driven from the public domain. The sacred, then, remains confined to the church and the secular becomes an autonomous sphere controlled by human reason.

Contrast the lives of children born in Christendom with those born in today's secular culture. In Christendom persons grew up believing that God had made the world, that the world was redeemed by Jesus Christ, and that the church guaranteed forgiveness and eternal life.

In the secular state none of these convictions prevail. The child of the secular society, without the benefit of the church, learns that creation came into being by accident for no apparent purpose. Bible and religion are excluded from the educational curriculum. In the U. S. culture this child will be exposed to perspectives on Christian faith through the newspaper, television, and perhaps through a friend or acquaintance. In adolescent years this child will hear about controversies concerning the use of public land for manger scenes, crosses, and public gatherings. From most of her friends she will learn that religion is a private affair that she can take or leave and that everyone's faith is his/her own business. Above all she will learn by hints, innuendoes, and suggestions that she should not speak about religion with anyone.

Perhaps the term "pagan," rather than "secular," more accurately depicts North American culture. It is increasingly pagan, exchanging God for alternative gods like pleasure, wealth, and social status. The modern preoccupation with sexuality and physical possessions parallels the pagan worship of fertility and the earth. "...For though they knew God, they did not honor him as God or give thanks to him, but they became futile in their thinking, and their senseless minds were darkened" (Rom. 1:21).

The church must now assume that persons who attend its functions do not even know the basics of the Christian faith – Bible stories, the meaning of baptism, the Lord's supper, or Christian commitment. Providing basic information about the faith and a Christian lifestyle proves imperative.

Thesis #9
The culture is also pluralistic with every competing view of life and the world standing on equal footing; each view is considered equally good and no one has the right to question the view of another.

"Pluralism," or the belief that more than one universal principal exists, dominates contemporary life. Each person may choose from the smorgasbord. While one person believes that being a good human being fulfills the purpose in life, another believes the spiritual experience of the New Age philosophy offers the greatest hope for the future. Others immerse themselves in Transcendental Meditation or follow Buddhism, Hinduism, or Islam. Perhaps mixed in the swirl of beliefs stands a Christian who believes that Christ is the Way, the Truth, and the Life (John 14:6).

In a pluralist culture, "As long as the Church is content to offer its beliefs modestly as simply one of the many brands available in the ideological supermarket, no offense is taken. But the affirmation that the truth revealed in the gospel ought to govern public life is offensive."[9]

Most Christians believe that we are not alone in the universe, that we have not been left to our own devices but that we can depend upon God. Though we believe this, we must have the integrity to publicly testify that we have chosen this place to stand. We have stepped into the tradition of

Jesus Christ and accepted him as the standard of truth about God and humanity. He provides the "clue to history" which makes the human story meaningful.[10] He offers the way for humanity to live in relation to God and to each other.

When we acknowledge the ground on which we stand, we are free to make our witness and to engage other persons on this basis. Those to whom we witness have the right to ask us the basis for our claims and we must have the courage and commitment to speak of our way of being in the world. While this may sound less "absolute" than we would prefer, it is, I believe, both honest and faithful. Having acknowledged our particular choice and the reasons for it, we then have the right to ask of others on what basis they take their stands.

In this kind of environment the church must prepare itself for ministry at the threshold of the twenty-first century.

THESIS #10
Because the electronic media has become the dominant mode of communication the church must discover how to minister to a visual culture.

By the age of 20, today's American has watched an average of 22,000 hours of television. The new generation learns through the eyes as much as through the ears.

The communication explosion began about 1950. Until then communication occurred mostly through print and sound. In the years of World War II, movies carried visual news reports but little communication took place through television.

Since 1950 each year has added new layers of visual communication. First came television in major cities with persons on the fringe of the broadcast area receiving snowy pictures in black and white. From the poorest homes to the richest, shacks and mansions proudly displayed their TV antennas as tangible evidence they had joined the information age.

Soon came the birth of cable, which made television accessible to persons in remote areas. With the advent of cable persons were no longer confined to two or three major network channels and perhaps an educational or an independent channel. Cable not only made television available to remote areas, with choices of several channels, but it soon added other features, making the variety of programs almost limitless. Now instead of reading books, newspapers, and news magazines, the new generation watches TV.

Concurrent with the growth of cable reception came the satellite. With this innovation, instant, visual, worldwide communication became a reality. Television brought the Vietnam War into living rooms with daily reports of losses and shifts of strategy. Later, the Gulf War became the first to be fought on TV.

Increasingly, video is becoming not only an entertainer but also a playmate for Americans as interactive technologies grow. Today's home video games will soon give way to tomorrow's interactive programming, allowing viewers to manipulate and even create what they view. Likewise, "virtual reality" will become the drug of the wealthy as technology continues its incursion into reality.

When a child has had the television for a baby sitter, an instructor, and an entertainer for 18 or 20 years, how will this affect the way that person learns? Perhaps we should be aware that this person not only learns through pictures but learns in short bytes with frequent changes of images. This subtle instructor has told our children (in advertisements) that they should have the best, have it when they desire it, and have as much of it as they like. Corporate advertisers have spent billions of dollars to plant these messages in the subconscious of the "Now" generation. The church must choose its response to this visual generation that believes it deserves the best of everything, the instant it desires it.

PERSPECTIVE ON
PARTICULAR CHURCHES

THESIS #11
*Mainline churches have been disestablished in the prevailing culture
and continue to decline in numbers and influence.*

From the adoption of the U.S. Constitution church and state
have been separated in American culture. In the early days of the
nation this separation meant that churches neither received funding from
the state nor were under the control of elected officials - as in Europe
where churches were supported by taxes and worked in conjunction with
the state.

Even though this legal separation existed, society respected the
church for its Christian values. Prayer and Bible reading were the norm in
schools. Prayers were offered "in the name of Jesus" at public gatherings
and civic meetings. The religious dimension of the culture confronted the
unchurched at every turn.

In addition to these cultural manifestations of the church in secular
culture, the church provided leaders for the nation. To elect a man to
Congress who was neither a believer nor generally active in the life of a
congregation was unthinkable.

The changing role of the mainline church in the culture may be but a
minimal facet of the decline in numbers. But the major causes of the dra-
matic decline are (1) the decision of many Baby Boomers not to return to
church after college, (2) the changed agenda of mainline churches to
focus on social issues to the neglect of ministry to persons, and (3) the
fact that most mainline denominations did not adapt to the cultural
changes.

In the words of Loren Mead, "The culture that used to pretend to
teach faith no longer does so, but the congregation has not discovered
patterns and disciplines for nurturing either its people or newcomers to
the faith."[11]

THESIS #12
Congregations today have their ministry in a missionary situation without the previous supports to which they had become accustomed.

The "missionary situation" of the mainline churches has been precipitated by the disestablishment of their role in the culture and the growth of secularism. Both of these changes resulted from the breakdown in the church/culture synthesis.

Before the disestablishment of the church in American culture, Christians expected public schools to introduce children to scripture and prayer. Christians expected their values to be received with appreciation. They expected government to pass laws favorable to the endeavors of the church, like exemption from taxes and tax credits on gifts to the church. Ministers were excluded from military service.

Compare that favorable environment to the treatment Christianity popularly receives today in the entertainment media. More often than not they stereotype a clergy person either as a dope buried in religious jargon who knows nothing about the real world or as a huckster who professes faith while stealing money or seeking illicit sexual liaisons.

These shifts in the American culture point to the demise of a "Christian" nation with a mission to be the "New Israel," a light to the world. Rather, America is pagan and comprises a new mission field. If the church gives witness in such a missionary situation, the old ways of ministry will not work. The failure to note this change explains the frustration many pastors and church leaders experience while they perpetuate old forms of ministry with decreasing results.

THESIS #13
Most congregations remain totally unprepared to cope with the changed situation and as a consequence continue to decline.

Congregations are unprepared to cope with the new situation in American culture, largely because the change has been sudden and swift. The change came veiled as progress, freedom, and human rights and was not interpreted as the disintegration of the culture nor as an attack upon the church.

Mainline churches have difficulty coping with these cultural changes because they threaten power and control. Too many congregations doggedly maintain old structures because these structures keep the same persons in power.

Denominational bureaucracy contributes to the stagnancy of local congregations by rationalizing existing programs and structures. Seminaries support the status quo by continuing to train maintenance-minded ministers.

William Easum likens these stagnant denominations to dinosaurs. "Both have great heritages. Both require enormous amounts of food. Both influenced their world tremendously. And both became endangered species. Perhaps dinosaurs became extinct because of their unwillingness or inability to see what was happening all around them."[12]

Will the mainline church recover from its loss of touch with reality?

THESIS #14
A disproportionate number of congregations face discouragement from their failure of mission and dissension arises between church leaders and pastors.

When a vision fails, both pastors and members feel deceived. The 1950s nurtured the great hope that the church would pervade American life and culture, that family values would prevail, and that the institution would continue to prosper and grow. To support this vision, men and women gave millions of dollars in money and much more in volunteer service. Churches multiplied and memberships grew for a couple decades.

Now the 1950s vision has failed. New neighbors, quite different from those who lived around us 40 years ago, have moved next door. Our way of being the church seems foreign to them: the music does not appeal to them; they don't understand the liturgy; and, they don't measure up to the social standards that we unofficially set for our members. Those who built the church are older now. They do not want to change worship, dress code, language, or liturgy. So, they do not give the warmest welcome to those "unlike" themselves.

With dwindling membership, tight budgets, and a growing number of persons surviving on fixed incomes, older leaders hold the line on changes by doing what they have always done. They seem to think that doing the old programs better in increasing volume will restore the church to its 1958 heyday.

James Hudnut-Beumler suggests that life in the church will never again be like it used to be. "We can no longer hope to return to the church life of the 1950s. If we continue to play that game we are doomed."[13]

When the old strategy doesn't work and change does not represent a viable option, many church leaders grow frustrated to the point of exploding. And they do! They attack the minister, other members, and the denomination. As a result, about 40 percent of small churches have had a major conflict in the last three years, and 25 percent of large churches have been split, angry, and in major conflict.[14]

THESIS #15
Mainline denominations are experiencing the judgment of God
intended for our correction and redirection.

At first, this pronouncement may seem harsh. Who can say with certainty that specific situations or consequences should be called the "judgment of God"? If we think of "judgment" as God's evaluation of our vision and action, this idea takes away the sting of a vindictive, arbitrary pronouncement.

This assertion of God's judgment does not rest solely upon the church's loss of place or numerical and financial decline. In part the vitality of the Spirit and sacrificial service seem to be missing in many mainline churches. Seminal aspects of the gospel do not inform our mission.

Judgment also takes the form of confusion and conflict as at Babel (Gen. 11:1-9). The church bears scars from conflicting positions on abortion, sexuality, and mission because we lack a common vision.

God's judgment might also be revealed in the fact that our own children have not returned to the church. The judgment feels heavy when we see our offspring in exile far from home. Receiving baptized persons from other churches and denominations does not ease the pain of our lost children.

The judgment of God invites us to repent, change! We must change our minds about God, about the church, about the future!

THESIS #16
Most congregations are in dire need of transformation
and revitalization which includes:

▶ A Recovery of a Sense of the Presence of God,

▶ A Shift from 'Maintenance' to Mission,

▶ The Revitalization of Worship,

▶ The Liberation of the Laity,

▶ The Selection and Nurturing of Mentors,

▶ The Formation of Small, Intentional Groups.

These six dimensions of church life have been lost, unbalanced, or neglected in many congregations. Of course rarely has a church lost all of these seminal characteristics; churches can seldom exist without possessing at least some of them.

These six phases constitute the basic elements of being a church. We cannot be a church without the Presence of God in our midst. Worship centers on the praise of this God who creates and sustains us. God is for everyone and should be worshiped in ways that allow all persons to participate.

Many congregations focus on the grace of Christ: the power to heal, to remember, to bless; the power to do justice and love mercy and walk humbly with God."[15]

Laity will be best prepared for ministry through small groups in which persons are mentored in the faith and discern their spiritual gifts.

We cannot accurately predict a structure for Future Church. Life begets structure, not the other way around. The recovery of these essential dynamics of the church's life will merely prelude the birth of Future Church.

THESIS #17
Mainline churches need to recover a sense of the Presence of God
in their life and ministry.

Many churches seem to operate very well without God. Consider how much or little time a typical minister spends alone in prayer listening for the guidance of God. What role does spiritual discernment play in crucial decisions? If one should ask members why they go to church, how many would say, "To worship God"?

In the pre-missionary days of American culture the church experimented with various forms for its life. First, it wanted the minister to be a scholar who knew a bit more than others in the congregation, at least about the Bible and church history. Then entered the pastoral care movement, turning ministers into therapists. In reaction to authoritarian "God talk," clinical pastoral education made it clear ministers were never to bring up the subject of "God" unless signaled by the client.

As the therapist model wore thin, the management model came forward to define an achievable goal. "Mystery and mess are eliminated at a stroke."[16] When not needed or consulted, God seldom appears. We blind ourselves to the Presence of God among us.

When there is no sense of the Divine, people go home empty. Soon they forget the main reason for church and worship. As the awareness of God withers, joy evaporates and persons find it increasingly difficult to speak of God to one another.

Before today's church members can discern their mission and engage in serving God in the world, they need to recover a sense of God in their corporate and personal lives. Two great symbols stand in every sanctuary: the communion table and the baptismal font. Symbolically, congregation members need to stand at the font and recall their own baptism. Each has been baptized into Jesus Christ; each has been joined to the other in his body.

And with a new awareness we need to take his body and his blood, knowing that these mediate to us the life and the Spirit of Jesus. The empowerment for mission derives from the presence of Jesus whom we meet in the bread and the wine.

Prayer cannot be divorced from baptismal renewal or Eucharistic feeding. Prayer exists at the heart of both. But beyond these liturgical forms of prayer congregations and serious believers need to pray for the Lord of the church to be evident in the water, the bread and wine, the preached word, and the living fellowship of the Spirit.

THESIS #18
We need to recover the conviction that church is about God and a people – a people who love, worship, and obey God.

The church is not bricks and mortar; it is not a denomination nor an institution. The church is not a lobbying group. The church is the Body of Jesus Christ on earth (1 Cor. 12:27).

People make up the church; the church is the people. But not just any people. The church consists of those persons who have been baptized into Jesus Christ by the Spirit, who are nurtured by his body and blood, and who share in his mission to the world.

The primary focus for this community centers on "being," on who we are. What we do flows out of our unique identity as the People of God. Because we are a "called" people we worship, pray, obey, and serve God in the spirit of Jesus Christ.

In Future Church we will learn the ways of God more clearly because the culture will force us to claim faith purposefully. In that day we will not be embarrassed to call upon God to show us our mission and to empower us for a task we can neither organize, manipulate, nor make happen. In that day we will experience the amazing power of God to fulfill the mission of Christ in the world.

THESIS #19
When the church prays, it postures itself to hear what the Lord of the church will say.

The most direct and immediate way into "a sense of the Divine Presence" comes through prayer, the natural posture of the church. By prayer the church was born (Acts 1:14); through prayer the church is nurtured; by prayer the church receives guidance; with prayer the church gains empowerment.

"Prayer is the pivot action in the Christian community...Praying is a joining of realities, making a live connection between the place we find ourselves and the God who is finding us."[17]

Nothing supersedes prayer in importance. Indeed, more than new programs, the church most needs a new commitment to pray. We do not need more information about prayer; we need to pray. In prayer we set our minds and hearts upon the presence of God, not the gifts of God.

Imagine a denomination becoming so serious about God that it sets aside a Sunday to do nothing but pray. Picture every church in every community with even one-half its members praying for the Divine Presence to invade their lives, congregations, and the country. How changed would be our ministry!

Thesis #20
We need to repent with the assurance that God chooses to
be revealed to the congregation that turns from its own way
to the way of God.

For some, the feelings associated with repentance still carry the
sting of false confessions, drummed up emotions, or anguished
pounding upon one's chest. Though such styles of repentance have had
their place, we are thinking of another type of repentance.

Christian repentance derives from the Greek term *metanoia*, which
means "to turn around, to change one's mind." The church requires this
kind of repentance today – a change of mind about who we are, where we
are in the culture, what our task must be if we are to be faithful.

God is grieved with our blindness; God is grieved with our misdirec-
tion; God is grieved with our barrenness. On each occasion when the
people of God have repented, God has "heard from heaven, forgiven their
sin, and healed their land" (2 Chron. 7:14). With the conviction that
God's gracious nature can be counted upon, let us repent.

Thesis #21
The rebirth of the church occurs through encounters with
God and the world God has created.

The rebirth of the church means a renewal of the dynamic energy
of the Spirit, operative in the life and mission of the congregation.
Energy evaporates when the worshipping Body of Christ substitutes form
and tradition for a vital encounter with the Living God. When this sub-
stitution occurs, form becomes idolatrous and insulates the church from
transformative contact with the Divine Presence.

The way of recovery begins with an encounter with God, which can
occur in seemingly unlimited ways. God comes to us through the reading
and preaching of the Word, through the administration of the sacraments, through consecrated and serious prayer, and also in serendipitous,
unpredictable ways.

When the Spirit comes, old visions are shattered along with any old
forms that no longer mediate the Divine Presence. Wonder, awe, and
mystery accompany the breaking in of the Spirit. A community infused
with the Spirit possesses a focus, an energy, and a commitment that cannot be achieved by human technique or manipulation.

The church in the power of the Spirit discerns the Spirit's work in the world, particularly in the pain of persons outside its walls. When the church through the Spirit responds to needs of persons in the culture, the kingdom of God takes shape in its ministry. In these daring acts of receptivity and engagement with God and God's world the church is renewed.

THESIS #22
Women are bringing a renewed sense of the Spirit and a model for authentic spirituality to congregations.

The growing leadership of women in church renewal hints at the Spirit's activity. Women are awakening congregations to the Spirit and providing models of spirituality.

Why would the intervention of women in the life and leadership of the church bring about spiritual renewal? Perhaps women often have greater sensitivity to the inner world of the Spirit than their male counterparts. More women pray. They tend to exhibit less need to compete or to win. Perhaps these stereotypes of women hold some truth.

In distinguishing males and females some theorists suggest that most males seek power, while most women aim to establish relationships. And relational leadership has always been in harmony with the gospel of the Lord who called us "friends" (John 15:15).[18]

Perhaps, women have been encouraged to draw upon the Spirit to face the resistance of male-dominated institutions. Both historically and currently, they face bastions of power under male control, and the dominant do not easily relinquish their position. What's more, unlike men, most women do not hide behind a hard exterior, hungering to win, to achieve, and to compete.

Whether liberal or conservative, whether involved in evangelism or social activism, concerned women ministers recognize the need for prayer and contemplation. Whether their theological and missional commitments point to a witness for Christ or service to the poor, a deep sensitivity to the Spirit energizes both.

THESIS #23
The churches of the mainline must shift from a maintenance mentality to a missional passion.

This shift comes about through a renewed engagement with the Spirit and the church's context. Without the movement of the

Spirit this shift will be nothing more than manipulation of a congregation through managerial tactics - a strategy that has failed to renew congregations in the Spirit.

A maintenance mentality bears multiple characteristics that make it easy to recognize. First, a maintenance mentality has a past orientation. Everything is measured by the golden age of the 1950s when pews were filled with people, the budget was easily raised, and excitement reigned.

Maintenance-oriented congregations are defensive and resistant to change. Any questioning of church practices meets with harsh criticism. For the maintenance-minded congregation the status quo represents the ideal for past, present, and future. Because "the way things are" meets the needs of persons presently in the church, it should not be questioned and will not be changed. A congregation may even recognize its need to change, yet resist and feel threatened when change is initiated - even when many members are in favor of it.[19]

The curse of blindness proves more devastating for this congregation. It remains blind to its context. Often, the neighborhood around a church has changed racially, socially, and economically; it may have become more commercial, fallen into disrepair, or simply aged. In spite of such changes many congregations continue their ministry in old, familiar ways. Finally, the maintenance congregation believes the lie that familiar, tested programs always produce the same results. Someone has said, "If you keep on doing what you have always done, you will get more of what you've already got." The church suffers from the illusion that it can recover its past glory. The truth: this church will never be like it was 40 years ago. Never! The context has changed, the church has changed, the people have changed, and nothing will bring back the good old days.

THESIS #24
Most congregations revere the past more than they anticipate the future.

Congregations that "marry" their past seek security. While everything around the church has changed – the people, the community, and the opportunities for growth - members of a particular congregation recall the past as the "golden age" and they long to return to those days of certainty, success, and fulfillment. The way the church ministered in the 1950s seemed good and right. With the passing of time the style seems even better and more faithful.

The congregation's resistance to change does not constitute pure stubbornness but rather an effort to preserve meaning for persons who built the church and who have worshiped in it for years. The old ways give members stability in the midst of radical changes.

The yearning to return to the past dies hard. Even though the congregation cannot return to the success of yesterday, it refuses to adapt to present realities and falsely labels its resistance to change as the preservation of integrity.

While the past offers security and satisfaction, it blinds the church to the future. Even though the church cannot achieve the same numbers, interest, or participation of the past era, it can engage the present and move into a new, alternative future. The future stands open. Obedience to Christ leads the congregation into a creative and productive future.

THESIS #25
A past orientation leads to the repetition of old programs and practices that do not take into account the changed context.

When a congregation with no youth calls a youth minister in hopes of restoring a youth ministry, it repeats an old strategy in hopes of replicating past results.

When the membership has declined for 30 years and the church hires a minister of evangelism in hopes of enlisting new members, it is the last gasp of a dying church.

When the church institutes a food pantry and a clothes closet to serve new low-income residents in the community, it often makes an effort to be relevant without making the necessary radical changes.

When a congregation insists on classical music for a culturally deprived neighborhood, it serves itself rather than those outside the church.

When a congregation fails to open its facilities to neighborhood groups, it clearly indicates its intention to remain isolated from the real issues of pain and hope in the community.

THESIS #26
Repetition of old forms leads to veneration and finally to the sacralization of form without substance.

Adherence to church forms and structures born in the boom of the 1950s seems natural to those shaped by them. Once those forms and structures were relevant to the needs of the people in the church. Now they minister to a few who remain but ignore the needs of outsiders seeking hope.

Persons who adhere to old forms identify the forms with the substance, the truth of the faith. For example, when congregations sing "Come Thou Fount of Every Blessing" the words communicate the grace of God, and the music stirs the Spirit. What's more, after three generations a hymn takes on a life of its own; because it has served the sacred, it now has become sacred. Now suppose this wonderful, old hymn means nothing to new persons who join our worship. Because this hymn has come to be regarded as sacred in itself, those who introduce new music and different hymns get accused of betrayal and unfaithfulness to God.

Other untouchable, sacred objects may include the hymnal, the communion table or pulpit, choir robes, programs, or even seats in the sanctuary. Touch not! Change not!

Thesis #27
The tradition of too many churches is sacrosanct and therefore is defended and preserved at all costs.

The tradition of a church points to the manner of worship, the election of officers, the celebration of Advent, the role of the minister, etc. When the form becomes sacred, the Sacred suffers abuse.

One congregation informs the new minister that, "The liturgy we use has been in the church for 100 years and we do not expect you nor anyone to change it." Sacrosanct liturgy.

A congregation has for decades required ushers to dress in black suits and split tails and they expect to maintain this formality for another century or two.

Another congregation has sung "My Country Tis of Thee" as part of worship for 30 years. When the liturgy excludes this custom, complaints abound.

_One church governing body spent more time arguing about the removal of a bench from the front lawn of the church than they did considering feeding the hungry three blocks away.

The idea of changing the name of a church to create greater openness to outsiders created so much controversy, it was dropped from the agenda.

Simple. Silly? Foolish. Stubborn? Blind! How do you judge?

THESIS #28
Because of the veneration of the past many congregations resist any change in form, vision, and mission.

Form points to structures that give order to a congregation; vision indicates the way a church views the future; and mission addresses how a congregation expends energy in service. When the past enslaves a congregation, it cannot adapt to changes in context. As a result it becomes increasingly irrelevant.

What makes eleven o'clock on Sunday morning more sacred than 7 p.m. Saturday night? If worship was originally set at 11 a.m. to accommodate the milking schedule of farmers, why should a highly urban, mobile culture be bound to that time for worship? Given this history, why would a community consider the change to another hour irreverent? If Christ entered history and is Lord of all time, then all time has been hallowed by God.[20]

If Christ has risen from the dead and lives forevermore, why are we afraid of death? I speak not only of personal death but of the death of old visions for our lives and the life of the congregation. Theologian Jurgen Moltmann claims that Christ comes to us out of our future. If the point of Christ's coming lies before us, should we not look with expectation toward the future rather than to the past with regrets?

Our faith story, when rightly remembered, points the church toward the future. "The living remembrance of Christ directs the church's hope towards the kingdom…for it is not of their own strength, reason and will that people believe in Jesus as the Christ and hope for the future as God's future."[21]

To re-present Christ marks the mission of the church, and the hurt, pain, and need of persons around us tell us what we must do to actualize his re-presentation in the lives of people.

THESIS #29
Congregations that refuse to change are destined to die and further fuel the decline of mainline churches.

A congregation cannot live on tradition! It cannot live by looking only to the past while ignoring the present and the future. If it persists in this orientation it is bound to die.

Some congregations die before they are dead! Their living faith in Christ dies. Their vision of the future dies! Their hope to be more than a product of culture dies.

If a congregation does not open itself to "strangers" (those persons unlike the membership) it only bides time until the members get older, fewer, and eventually non-existent. Churches either grow or die. They cannot remain static. They cannot perpetuate their lives without receiving new persons.

Staid congregations with a survival mentality draw tightly together and close the entrances to new persons. The boundaries separating members from newcomers may be very obvious to a visitor, but invisible to those who create the boundaries.[22] Even when persons visit the church for worship or study, they do not find a place and eventually cease to come.

How can a church that refuses to welcome new persons – adapting and responding to their culture and needs – hope to survive?

Thesis #30
To foster new life, stagnant congregations must embrace the reality of their present context and imagine their life in new forms.

Churches that intend change must depend upon the presence of the renewing Spirit. Without the Spirit all human efforts to reorder an institution will fail.

When the Spirit comes three things are required for renewal of the congregation – the text, in context, with vision. The church is of God and thus depends upon God for its life. So it must turn to the Word of God to discover its identity and mission. This text, read under the illumination of the Spirit, quickens the church and informs the mission.

But the text must be read in context. When the text is read with those persons who now reside in the neighborhood of the church, the message of God will be heard with new ears. New people bring new needs and challenges to the congregation. By listening to these persons, the church interfaces the text with the context, helping to shape its mission.

A vision for the future comes as a gift of God. Through the interface of text with context, the old guard and the newcomers unite in the Spirit. Together, they imagine a vision that preserves the past and grasps the future. With this transformation the church need not die; it can and will live into the next generation as the people are faithful.

THESIS #31
The transformation required will be life-giving to some but will seem like death to others.

Radical changes which contain the seed of new life also deliver death to old forms that have outlived their usefulness. These changes liberate those who have been excluded, but they bring grief to those who have been at the center of power and control.

If the church moves from magnificent buildings to the lowly confines of a living room, those who have constructed and maintained the buildings will feel robbed. Those accustomed to the beauty of stained glass will see only the nakedness of clear bay windows. And they will grieve the loss, sensing their dream for the church has died.

As in any grief, the people may experience shock, depression, and anger before they find hope in the new reality.[23] New realities are plentiful these days.

For example, if the church opts to certify lay ministers, those who have spent years of study and preparation to fulfill a calling as ministers will experience the death of a dream. Yet, present day clerical paradigms did not dominate the early church and may lose power in Future Church.

When the form of ministry shifts from paternalism to participation, those who have held upper ranks in the church and social order will feel their position slipping away. And they, too, will grieve the loss.

Yet, when buildings no longer monopolize the Presence of God, common people will celebrate. When clergy no longer dominate the church, lay people will exult in their new freedom and responsibility. And, when the powerful lose control, the doors will be opened for the marginalized to participate in the life of the Body of Christ.

Future Church brings life to some but death to others, unless we all recognize our God-appointed place.

THESIS #32
Women have proved adept at revitalizing ineffective, declining, and often hopeless congregations.

The evidence mounts that many congregations declining in membership, vision, and sometimes hope have been rejuvenated by the ministry of women pastors. Why is it true?

Ministering to declining churches takes an understanding of process, a familiarity with pain, and a wealth of patience. According to Carol E.

Becker and other contemporary theorists, process, pain, and patience are part of women's experience. "Because their bodies give them graceful lessons in letting happen what needs to happen, women sometimes show a paradoxical strength as they embrace their vulnerability."[24]

Some people wonder if women have a special sensitivity to pain and suffering that makes them more effective ministers in waning congregations. The patience of many women enables them to face resistance and fear, helping frightened congregations to embrace change. The lack of competitiveness in some women enables them to share authority, empowering the laity for effective ministry.

Perhaps their effectiveness in ministering among marginal congregations may be credited to their special abilities to give birth and provide nurture. Is it true that some men also have these gifts for revitalization of lifeless congregations, gifts that often go unnoticed?

Whatever unique gifts women have that enable them to help struggling congregations, let the whole church be grateful. And let the whole church open its doors for the leadership of women in larger roles of vision and responsibility!

THESIS #33
All effective pastors (male and female) are destined to become more effective practical theologians who equip congregations to discern their mission in a changing world.

The church will move forward by equipping discerning people to make critical decisions about mission and ministry. While pastors have many responsibilities – preaching, teaching, guiding, and visiting the people - no task has greater significance than equipping leaders to discern and carry out the call of God in the church's life and mission.

True discernment requires that lay leaders be taught the faith – its biblical foundations, its historical struggles with culture, and the fundamental elements of spiritual discernment. Equipped with this training, chosen leaders become practical theologians who can recognize God's work both inside and outside the community of faith.

When the church dismisses theology in favor of the latest management fad, it loses the capacity for discernment and eventually presumes it does not even need God's gift to manage its ministry. With this shift to human ingenuity, leaders become managers, the church takes on the character of a business, and God becomes unnecessary.

According to theologian John Leith, "the renewal of the church is not hidden in the latest management jargon, theory, or technique, but in the study of the Bible, learning the theology of the church, and putting these into practice through acts of caring."[25]

Thesis #34
One key to the shift from maintenance to mission will be the change in orientation from program to persons.

Jesus' Great Commission, writes Stanley Ott, does not say, "go and start programs," but rather, "go and make disciples."[26] Programs are valuable only insofar as they nurture people in the spirit and image of Christ.

The shift from a program orientation to a people orientation requires a fundamental change in attitude. A church can run good and effective programs without personally caring for persons or sharing faith.

For example, a church may have a class for mothers of pre-school children to help them deal with parenting problems. This program, helpful as it may be, can be conducted by keeping the focus on the problems of young mothers. With this narrow focus, the program never addresses the deeper needs of the mothers: how they may grow in faith through the stresses of parenthood.

Person-focused ministry does more. A person-focused church, says Ott, more closely resembles a farm than a grocery store. A grocery store offers consumers many options, but nothing grows there. On a farm, in contrast, seeds are planted, nurtured, and brought to fruition. It is not necessary for a grocer (or a programmatic church) to be nurturing. But a good farmer (or people-centered church) nurtures and tends.[27]

Thesis #35
The biblical injunction "to make disciples" offers the most logical starting point for this reorientation of mission.

Disciple making requires a deeply personal form of ministry. It does not work toward the end of building the institution nor recruiting persons to do the work of the church nor even doing good works as an expression of our ethical life. Disciple making works toward the building of people.

We find the norm for a disciple in the person of Jesus. The apostle Paul discipled by encouraging others to imitate him as he imitated Christ

(1 Thes. 1:6). Who is Jesus Christ for the church? For the disciple? How we answer these questions about Jesus informs what it means to be a disciple.

We consider Jesus a "spiritual person" who lived with a sublime consciousness of the deeper dimension of life. He saw God active in all of creation, in the lives of persons, and in the unfolding of history. As "God with us," Jesus participated in the sacred dimension of life, and he invited others to enter into the Spirit and to become mediators of God's work in the world.

Shifting from program-centered ministry to person-centered ministry in order to make disciples requires us to explore ways of helping persons to hear and respond to the invitation of the Spirit. The focus on persons proves more crucial for ministry than church work or institutional repair.

Ultimately, all Christian ministry is person-centered because the person Jesus Christ, the lover of persons, is the "hub" of the church. "To receive God's self-revelation is not to know something we did not know before, but to know someone we did not know before."[28]

THESIS #36
The average congregation needs a revitalization of worship.

The worship of God is the central act of the church. In worship the church regularly turns toward the Sacred, opening itself to the reality of the Divine Presence through prayer, praise, and spiritual instruction.

Worship in which the congregation encounters God draws resources from the culture and converts them into sacred media for the divine/human interface in worship. Language, for example, derives from the culture and churches use the language of a culture to offer praise and instruction.

When the disparity between the language of the church and the surrounding culture becomes too great, the service of worship no longer speaks to outsiders. Yet, the coming of the Spirit at Pentecost enabled Christians to cross language barriers in proclaiming the gospel, and the Spirit still challenges God's people to speak in the language of the people.

The revitalization of worship will mean action on two fronts. First, members who unthinkingly follow the order must wake up. Though they know the vocabulary, the meaning escapes them.

Second, persons who know nothing about Christian worship may occasionally come to worship "looking" for the Sacred. To these persons, our worship often sounds like a foreign tongue. Either we must learn to speak their "language," or offer classes in our own. "The language that engages the person with no Christian memory won't sound sufficiently religious, or evangelical, or inclusive, or traditional…to some insiders."[29]

THESIS #37
The time, place, and manner of worship must be opened to critique in light of the kinds of persons to whom the church offers ministry.

Congregations which consist mainly of older persons who enjoy a traditional form of worship should not change. That is, they should not change if they do not intend to reach the generation born after 1950.

But, if the church has a vision for the future and intends to endure beyond its current membership, it must alter its form of worship. To begin with, younger persons structure time in a different manner. They often work five or six days each week, and on Sunday they travel, seek recreation, or rest. Saturday night rather than Sunday morning worship may provide an attractive option for them.

What is the setting of worship – sanctuary, fellowship hall, living room, or parlor? For many of the persons we label as secular or "liberal," the sanctuary of the Gothic cathedral seems formidable. They do not associate the formal place of worship with memories of the divine, of baptisms and weddings, funerals and Christmas celebrations. Many would prefer the intimacy of a small group, meeting in a living room or fellowship hall with the minister seated nearby in the circle, rather than enthroned in a pulpit. Such a model is actually closer to the early church's practice of propagating small, supportive house churches to provide "personal, Christian community in the midst of a hostile environment."[30]

Form refers to the liturgy. The Greek origin of our English word "liturgy" means the "work of the people." "In other words, [the term] is the quintessence of the priesthood of all believers in which the whole priestly community of Christians share."[31] The people of God in worship do the work of praise, confession, intercession, and listening. The liturgy outlines the way the people of God do their work.

All congregations have a liturgy. Even those who do not print a bulletin follow a basic pattern of worship. Whether "high" church or "low" church, those who attend learn the movements of worship.

If we aim to make worship accessible to the "uninitiated," we have two options: either we make worship accessible or we offer classes to the ignorant. The latter seems in many ways to deny the spirit and work of Jesus.

To make the necessary changes ministers will require the support of the congregation.

THESIS #39
The language of worship requires words, gestures, and sounds that are understood by the participants.

Church culture has a specialized language as do other sub-cultures like art, architecture, or physics. To converse intelligently in these fields a person must learn the language. Terms like *lines, shade, arches, particles, waves* and *hues* take on special meaning according to the environment.

Through two millennia the church has developed a specialized language using words like *incarnation, redemption, fall, reconciliation, sacrament,* and *witness.* Special words with special meaning! Words with long histories and layers of meaning are rarely appreciated by many who use them.

But these layers of meaning accumulate like a "process of sedimentation, dulling the edge and sapping the vitality of words. Good words, rich and evocative, tend to be overused, losing their elasticity and eventually becoming the stock in trade of comedians who mimic the caricatured preacher."[32]

If the language becomes obtuse to members, how can we expect the outsider to draw any significance from them? Simple substitutions of words can help the uninitiated to hear the Word and to worship.

THESIS #40
The service of worship should aim to incarnate the Presence of God in the culture and life of the worshipping people.

To incarnate means to "manifest in the flesh," as Jesus in his human flesh manifested the Presence of God. In Jesus, God walked into history, ate, laughed, befriended people, and suffered. The service of worship, likewise, in all of its parts aims to manifest God's presence.

Throughout the church's history, congregations have hammered out various cultural forms of worship that provide an opportunity to encounter the Living God. This liturgy has included praise, confession, listening to God, prayers of supplication and intercession, the offering of life, and the reception of God's blessing. These forms of worship provide focus, movement, and fullness to the worship of God.

While the formal aspects of worship have become stable, the content of worship must be "culture specific." For example, we draw the language of worship from the language of the people; the content of the prayers derives from the lives of the worshippers and the nature of God; the Word of the Lord is heard and interpreted in light of a particular context. If ministers avoid everyday language, writes Eugene Peterson, "we abandon the very field in which we have been assigned to work. Most of us, most of the time, are engaged in simple, routine tasks, and small talk is the natural language."[33]

Worship that lacks this kind of incarnational integrity leans toward Gnosticism, a form of worship that denies the connection between the spiritual realm and the everyday lives of people. While it may be pure in form, it lacks both the power to communicate and the power to transform. Vital worship in its long tradition preserves integrity and demonstrates cultural sensitivity.

THESIS #41
Music of praise to God can have variety, relevance, and contemporary appeal without losing its integrity.

No specific form of music should hold a monopoly on the worship and glorification of God! Consider music from an international context and one immediately breaks free of music composed in Europe in the eighteenth and nineteenth centuries. Classical compositions communicate with those who have "ears to hear," but they do not speak to the musically illiterate.

Musical changes create confusion and grief for long-time worshippers. Particular tunes have been their very breath for decades. These hymns have expressed their praise to God; in them they have heard the love and grace of God. The texts and melodies of hymns have been woven into the fabric of life. To give these up for unfamiliar words and tunes frustrates, confuses, and angers those faithful worshippers.

From another perspective, those who were not reared with these tunes lack connection with them. "Culturally relevant music can be discovered by determining what radio stations most of your worship guests (not members) listen to. Every survey will show that 'soft rock' is the music of the majority of unchurched people in America."[34] The songs that people hear every day on the radio or television stand in stark contrast with ancient classical hymns. In worship, the old tunes leave the unchurched cold.

If the church intends to reach persons with different cultural tastes, it must provide a musical language that newcomers understand and speak. Martin Luther and Charles Wesley both borrowed music from the taverns for their hymns in an effort to be culturally relevant. Whenever the church has been serious about including the outsider, it has always taken music from the culture to teach its theology and to provide joyous praise for the newly baptized.

THESIS #42
Whatever the language, style, or form, the service of worship aims to enable persons to encounter the presence of the Living God in praise, confession, and obedience.

Worship brings persons into the Presence of God and invites them to offer themselves to God. Christian worship, writes Professor Paul W. Hoon, includes a two-fold action: that of "God to the human soul in Jesus Christ and in [human] responsive action through Jesus Christ."[35]

Congregations do not change the forms of worship to become modern; they do not adopt a different kind of music so they will sound contemporary; they do not adopt a new style so the minister will appear more like one of them. Altering the pattern of worship has only one aim – to enable more people to worship God heartily and intelligently.

Revising the form of worship offers one way that a congregation keeps the worship of God alive and inclusive. Priest Ezra modeled this wisdom when he led worship for the Israelites who had returned to Jerusalem after a long exile in Babylon. He was careful to speak "clearly," explain the meaning of scripture, and guide them through movements of repentance, commitment, and celebration (Nehemiah 8).

Worship cannot be lively for those who do not understand it, and old forms may become so routine that worship occurs by rote and not from the heart. Changing, updating, and building in new cultural forms speaks to both these issues.

THESIS #43
Altering the worship of a congregation will prove to be the most challenging and risky change it faces.

Grant the thesis that our form of worship must be altered. Making this decision does not guarantee that the congregation can navigate its way through the dangerous rapids to a safe and harmonious place beyond the changes. Numerous challenges await the congregation committed to change.

First, congregations will face the challenge of maintaining the integrity of worship. In the struggle to be culturally relevant, many congregations will stray too far and sacrifice the heart of worship.

Second, some congregations will resist all efforts to change. Others will fail to negotiate the proper blend of old and new. Still other groups will adopt a ready-made form created by another church from a different context. All these shortcuts must be avoided if a congregation aims for a faithful form of contemporary worship.

Others will seek too much change too quickly! Congregations can absorb only so much change at a time. Someone has suggested that, at any given time, a group can handle only about thirty percent change; anything beyond that creates too much anxiety for the group.

Change also poses a three-fold risk for the congregation. First, the altered form of worship may not truly glorify God, when the chief purpose of worship is not to be contemporary but to facilitate faithful worship. If changes in worship do not glorify God, the pain of change has been for naught. Second, if the church changes its mode of worship and those who formerly felt excluded still feel excluded, the effort has been in vain. Finally, the church risks that even though the changes glorify God and include the outsiders, the "faithful" who provide the major support for the church will cease to contribute time and money.

George Hunter observes that "growing denominations are slow to change their theology and quick to change the cultural forms and styles in which they communicate their theology; declining denominations, however, are quick to change their theology and slow to change their forms and styles."[36]

Given the promise and perils involved, change should be undertaken with careful planning and deep sensitivity.

THESIS #44

The Laity —People of God — in Future Church will be liberated for ministry both in the church and in the world.

The church is the people. The people of God are God's ministers both in the church and in the world. One of the great errors of the pre-Reformation church occurred by narrowly defining the church as the clergy. When the church's authority and ministry reside only in the ordained ministry, the role of laity is reduced to observing the clergy proclaim the Word and administer the sacraments.

The Reformers, especially Martin Luther, emphasized the "priesthood of all believers." This emphasized that all baptized persons had access to the Word, to prayer, and to both elements of the sacrament of holy communion. All Christians, as members of a "holy priesthood," represent Christ to the world and share the task of proclaiming God's "mighty acts" (1 Pet. 2:9). For this reason, the ordained ministry was not elevated over the laity but was set apart for particular functions within the church.

Unfortunately, the Reformers never pressed this cardinal doctrine to its full maturity, and the authoritative preacher of the Word easily slipped into the authoritative role of the priest. With this easy assumption of clerical power and authority, the laity was again marginalized and reduced to passive involvement in the congregation. This reduction limited the authority of the laity to initiate and perform ministry in the world.

To be liberated, the laity must be allowed to claim their status as representatives of Jesus Christ in the church, workplace, and world. Congregations must recognize the place of the laity in leadership, worship, and ministry. The church must also equip them to fulfill their vocation in their secular appointments. For lay persons to fully grasp their authority radical changes must occur in most congregations and in the self-identification of most laity.

In Europe's Catholic Church, "the decline of the number of priests has led to efforts to find out how the laity can, in a given place, take on the responsibility of the life of the Christian community that no longer has a resident ordained minister."[37] The crisis of church decline in America provides a similar awakening as laity claim their responsibility for ministry.

THESIS #45
Every baptized person has a vocation in and through Jesus Christ.

Baptism immerses the individual believer into the Body of Christ. As a member of the Body of Christ, he or she has the full authority of a follower of Christ.

Each baptized person has been called to faith in Jesus Christ, including the conviction that Jesus is the Christ, the Son of the Living God. Believing in Jesus leads to baptism and inclusion in the community of faith. Or, for those already baptized, the response of faith claims all the benefits of baptism. As believers in Christ we are joined to him through the Spirit.

The baptized are called not only to believe, but also to participate in the life of the church. Christian faith recognizes individual believers primarily as part of the believing community. To be joined to Christ means that we are joined to everyone who is joined to him.

In this fellowship of the baptized each one is called to use his or her gifts for the benefit of all. The exercise of gifts in the body works "for the common good," building up others in the life of the faith community (1 Cor. 12:7).

The call or vocation of the members of the body cannot be limited to the sphere of the church; it also extends into the world, the secular sphere of business and industry, politics and education. The call to ministry in the secular sphere encounters resistance because most Americans (including many Christians) no longer believe that religious faith can help people deal with difficult issues in the "secular" areas of everyday life.[38]

THESIS #46
Each person possesses particular gifts for ministry.

When persons are baptized into the Body of Christ, the Holy Spirit gives them spiritual gifts which are consecrated to Christ. Gifts in the Body of Christ come from one of two sources: creation or redemption; nature or grace.

An examination of gifts in the Body of Christ suggests that some persons are created with certain gifts for the community. The gift of imagination, for example, seems to be a natural, inborn trait for some persons. When these persons are baptized, this gift of Christ in creation is consecrated and becomes an instrument of ministry in the community.

But other gifts seem to be the special gift of the Spirit through participation in the community. These gifts may not have been in evidence prior to the person's participating in a worshipping, supportive community. The community provides the setting for the emergence of these gifts. From scripture we learn that every Christian possesses a gift or gifts from Christ. *Charisma*, the Greek word meaning "divine gift" is closely related to *charis*, meaning "grace" or "undeserved favor." The undeserved gifts we receive from Christ must be used for the building up of the Body of Christ, not for one's own up-building (1 Cor. 12:7-11). The church of Jesus Christ never faces a shortage of resources!

THESIS #47
All baptized persons need support and guidance to claim and use their gifts for ministry in the church and in the world.

Persons become aware of the gifts of Christ through their own intuitions and the affirmation of the church. Some persons seem to be unaware of their gifts until someone else affirms them. Paul did this for Timothy by affirming his faith and encouraging him to exercise his gifts for leadership and teaching. Other persons intuitively notice the positive inner response and the positive effects that come when they perform certain tasks. Each of these awarenesses may point to the manifestation of a gift of the Spirit.

John Calvin wrote that all the gifts of the Spirit have their wellspring in the anointing of the Holy Spirit which Jesus received at his baptism. Baptism marks us as those with whom Christ shares the power of the Spirit.[39]

But even persons who begin to notice the work of the divine Spirit through impulses, surprising expressions accompanied by inner satisfaction, still require the community of discernment to verify their gifts. Such verification generally comes from the community through affirmations of tasks well done and through a "fit" between a person and task.

Sometimes the more subtle gifts of the Spirit, like discernment and faith, require cultivation through teaching and instruction. As persons with gifts engage scripture, the gifts rise to consciousness and mature in ways that may be shared with others.

Like any gift, spiritual gifts must be received. "Healthy churches push people into ministry where the Holy Spirit has gifted them rather than where the church organization needs them."[40] The Body of Christ finds fulfillment as the church receives these gifts and supports them.

THESIS #48
There is no qualitative distinction between ministry in the
church and ministry in the marketplace.

Before the Reformation, everyone understood the work of the
clergy (priests, bishops, the Pope, and religious orders) to be truly
"holy" because it had to do with the church, the sacraments, and the
Truth of God.

In the Reformation the terms "priest" and "ministry" were freed from
their narrow bounds. All laity were elevated to a new status of "priesthood"
and the arena for ministry became the world. During the Reformation
the new role of the laity was spelled out in theory but in practice it never
fully took shape. From the sixteenth century until today the church has
struggled to liberate the laity for effective ministry.

In Future Church we will recognize that the church is not to be the
primary recipient of the laity's service, but rather the vehicle for their service to the world – encompassing their homes, places of work, and the
political arena. Here, in these places, they witness for Christ in both a
personal and corporate manner.

French theologian Jacques Ellul said it well: "God became incarnate
– it is not for us to undo his work. This dissociation of our life into two
spheres – the one 'spiritual,' where we can be 'perfect,' and the other
'material' and unimportant, where we behave like other people – is one of
the reasons why churches have so little influence on the world."[41]

Only when the theology of the Kingdom exerts its rightful influence
upon the church will the church recognize its role as a spearhead of the
Kingdom. The Kingdom, life under God in every sector, will mean the
completion of the work of the church. Then our prayer will be answered,
"Thy Kingdom come, Thy will be done on earth as it is in heaven."

THESIS #49
A primary task of the ordained minister is the equipping of
the baptized for ministry.

Laity become effective in ministry only as they are informed and
empowered – equipped by those trained to give leadership. The
ordained minister has been appointed to equip the laity for ministry. The
author of the Epistle to the Ephesians wrote, "The gifts he gave were that
some would be apostles, some prophets, some evangelists, some pastors
and teachers, to equip the saints for the work of ministry, for building up

the body of Christ..." (Eph. 4:11-12).

"Equipping pastors have a vision and train people to bring about that vision...The equipping pastor does very little ministry. Instead the equipping pastor steps aside and encourages the laity to be ministers of the congregation."[42]

Equipping the laity, then, becomes the ordained minister's primary task. When baptized persons understand the scriptures and faith tradition, they can bring their particular issues of ministry into dialogue with the faith. In this dialogue between the workplace, Christian family, politics, and faith in Christ, these disciples sharpen their understanding of what it means to be a witness in every arena of life.

In addition to instruction the minister must also provide support to the laity. This means listening to their stories about successful and failed efforts to practice the faith. This requires the gifts of patience, encouragement, and assurance of forgiveness.

Lay ministers are empowered through worship, the sacraments, and spiritual nurture. Since the ordained have a primary responsibility for these churchly functions, they provide the setting for this empowerment. Obviously, however, clergy cannot provide spiritual power to the laity; this power comes only from God.

But effective clergy preach and lead worship in a manner that exposes people to God's truth. They administer the sacraments with an eye to the mission of the baptized in the marketplace. The minister enters into the struggles of the laity by listening, praying, and offering spiritual direction. In these ways faithful ministers offer spiritual empowerment to the ministry of lay persons.

THESIS #50
The laity in Future Church will claim their voice in the governance of the church.

Laity have never been entirely speechless in church governance, but their authority has too often been purchased with threats of withdrawal or withholding contributions. Their voice must speak in Future Church with new accents and affirmations.

Informed laity will bring a witness fueled with passionate conviction, informed by the scriptures and tradition, and proven in their everyday lives. Because their faith has been hammered out in their encounter with the world, these enlightened laity will speak the truth of God with integrity and persuasive power.

Issues that come before general church councils, assemblies, or conferences will no longer be dominantly addressed by clergy with vested interests. Rather, issues and solutions will be shaped by interested lay men and women who have a strong investment in the church and its mission to the world.

THESIS #51
The church must be intentional about developing spiritual mentors who model, nurture, and pass on the faith to children and secular seekers.

A spiritual mentor knows the faith, has matured in the faith, and practices the gift of passing on the faith to others. The image of the mentor is reflected in the practice of the early church. When outsiders came to the church seeking admission, they were not immediately baptized. Instead, these "inquirers" were placed under the care of a sponsor, or mentor.

The inquirer met with the mentor regularly for one or two years. In addition, the inquirer attended church services and listened to the singing, the preaching, and the teaching. When the mentor discerned that the inquirer was properly prepared, the inquirer was presented to the congregation as a candidate for baptism.

The mentor taught the inquirer how to live the Christian life. The mentor did not focus on theological purity but on lifestyle formation. This spiritual guide taught relationally by modeling practices, values, and lifestyle – the Christian Way.

Baptism and discipleship must go hand in hand. According to theologian Jurgen Moltmann, "Baptism joins a fragmentary and incomplete human life with the fullness of life and the perfect glory of God. Without new fellowship in a supporting group, this way cannot be pursued by individuals."[43]

Future Church will examine the meaning of baptism and likely change many of the traditional and cultural practices.

THESIS #52

Most congregations tend to reproduce themselves in the form of cultural Christians, blurring the distinction between prevailing cultural norms and the Christian lifestyle.

Christians in the "Constantinian" church (i.e., most mainline denominations) receive their formation by participating in the church's worship and program life. Most congregations assume that the baptized already know the essentials of the faith, that they have committed themselves to Christ, and that nurture will produce mature disciples.

But the church is only one of many forces seeking to shape persons. Schools, mass media, friends, and organizations all promote the prevailing beliefs and morals of the culture.

Christian educator C. Ellis Nelson writes, "If our first allegiance is to Christian beliefs, then our strategy is to develop the congregation into a community where morals are the practical expression of Christian beliefs."[44] Every element of the congregational ethos, from sermons to social events, must model distinctly Christian belief and lifestyle.

Yet, a close look at most congregations reveals much more Western American culture than radical Christian faith. If one asks any particular congregation what distinguishes members from those outside, the church is often hard pressed to answer with concrete examples of changed, radically committed lives.

The overlap between culture and the ethos of most churches produces a religious version of the culture. At its worst, the church baptizes and legitimates the values and lifestyle of the culture, passing it off for Christian discipleship. In fact, many of the baptized would feel embarrassed to be publicly identified as serious disciples of Jesus.

In his first epistle Peter speaks of the church as "a peculiar people" (1 Pet. 2:9). Although God-centered living may seem peculiar to the secular culture, the original Greek word means "claimed as a possession" of God. We live different lives because we have a different owner.

The way of change might begin with a mentorship that pairs each new member with a spiritually mature member for one year. During this year the mentor would guide the inquirer in establishing a Christian lifestyle.

Thesis #53

As the new millennium dawns, leaders of congregations need to define what it means to be "Christian" in a secular age and formulate plans for developing mentors of "apostolic" Christianity.

If we take mentorship seriously, the issue of a Christian lifestyle becomes paramount. Into what kind of lifestyle does the mentor guide the inquirer? While no one can define this goal for a congregation or a denomination, some suggestions may help.

The Christian lifestyle must be both scriptural and contextual. To have scriptural integrity a particular congregation/denomination must examine the demands of discipleship set forth in scripture. The teachings of Jesus and the model of his life present us with foundational material for discernment. God works through scripture to teach, reprove, correct, and train disciples (2 Tim. 3:16).

Discipleship must also be contextual. What discipleship issues does modern, secular culture present to us? Without being exhaustive, the list must at least include the environment, consumerism, sexual ethics, justice to the poor and marginalized, and the worship of God. When we see these issues through Jesus' call to a radical life of "love of God and love of neighbor," we must search for ways of holy obedience. The congregation must struggle with these issues and make some hard decisions. How should we live on this planet as we enter a new millennium?

Commitment to Jesus Christ "involves a real – even a radical – change in the life of the believer, which carries with it moral responsibilities that distinguish Christians from 'outsiders' while at the same time stressing their obligation to those 'outsiders.'"[45]

Perhaps the church's greatest challenge will be to define these responsibilities in a manner that escapes legalism and absolutism. Balance, flexibility, freedom, and intentionality may provide the mix of emphases for adopting a new way of life that manifests the gospel.

Thesis #54

To fulfill this task the church must issue the call and provide the training to equip effective spiritual mentors.

Those struggling with issues of contemporary Christian lifestyle will mentor others. Having struggled with the gospel in the modern context, these persons will have already begun the task of incarnational thinking, praying, and living.

Mentoring has always been the Christian method of perpetuating faith, whether through faithful mothers, sensitive pastors, or effective teachers. The tradition of mentoring has deep roots in the Christian tradition, perhaps beginning with Jesus who called twelve persons into a mentoring relationship. This method was continued by the apostle Paul who took Silas and others on missionary journeys.

The desert fathers and mothers mentored many who came to the desert, and the way of mentorship was institutionalized in the monastic movement beginning in the fourth and fifth centuries. Much later mentoring was called "spiritual direction" and made a standard practice among Jesuits. In various forms this ancient practice has been embraced by the churches of recent decades.

"The monastics assumed...that from the beginning of the Christian life to its end we are deeply dependent on fellow Christians...We must continually ask for and receive help from others. Consultation (mentorship) is the virtue that enables us to do so."[46]

The literature of this ancient practice provides many insights for the cultivation of mentors for a Church that longs for integrity and faithfulness in its present exile.

THESIS #55
One responsibility of a mentor will be to assume oversight of the People of God.

Laity have a ministry both inside and outside the congregation. The strength of the witness *without* depends upon the integrity of the life *within* the congregation. Paul took special care of congregational life because he was convinced that the congregation's unity, inclusiveness, spiritual vibrancy, and integrity of lifestyle provided evidence of the Kingdom Age that had begun with the resurrection of Jesus.

Like Paul, spiritual mentors must watch over (not control) the life of the Body of Christ. If the church's life is not distinct from the culture and does not manifest the Kingdom, its witness will be diluted. Like watchmen on the wall of the city, caring mentors are vigilant in prayer and in looking after the needs of the people (Isaiah 62:6).

In some ways a leader is like a jet pilot. "Just as the pilot and the cockpit crew are the only ones who can keep an eye on all the gauges, lights, warning systems, and procedures at the same time, so also the pastor and leadership team are in a position to keep an eye on the entire congregation, with its many operations."[47]

With the gentleness of Christ and the persistence of Paul these men and women of God will care for the church as a bride for her groom or a husband for his wife. Caring will be the glue that holds Future Church together in its integrity.

Thesis #56
In the twenty-first century the evangelistic task of the church will be accomplished in part through spiritual mentors. (Christianity has always been better caught than taught!)

Evangelism at its heart involves passing the faith on to a new generation or to a generation that has bailed out on the church. In either case these persons do not know or embrace the faith and need effective guidance in the art of Christian believing and living.

"Art" stands in contrast with "mechanics." For too long belief has been more mechanical than artistic. We have given persons the creed, the confessions, or the proper texts and requested their assent to these faith formulations. But, if we understand Christian believing as an art, we make room for intuition and imagination, for individuality and spontaneity. Art involves the whole person and not merely the rationality of the person. "We are his workmanship, created for good work in Christ" (Eph. 2:10).

Mentors will welcome these new persons into the community, get to know them, and build a relationship with them. "Although we may not be our brothers' and sisters' keepers, we are our brothers' and sisters' brothers and sisters. In other words, being persons is possible only if we are in community."[48] As a faithful brother or sister, the mentor learns to foster an environment in which faith and imagination can be released. Mentorship creates a chain reaction as new members become people who "will be able to teach others as well" (2 Tim. 2:2).

Thesis #57
The best way to initiate the needed transformations in the church will be through the formation of small, intentional groups —cadres of apostolic believers!

Small groups offer one way to launch congregational renewal and a shift from a management to a missional approach. The small, intentional group is not set apart from the congregation as special, elect, or superior in discipleship. Such elitism causes division and resentment among the people of God. Instead, small groups come from the congregation, represent the congregation, and seek to spearhead change in behalf of the congregation.

The life fostered in the small group eventually shapes the character of a congregation. The small group proves to be an ideal testing ground for the whole congregation when leadership wishes to experiment with new curricula or ideas. When discoveries come they can be shared; when failures occur they will not be devastating. The small group serves as an experimental task force.

The intentional group serves three purposes. First, it provides a place for the pastor to find retreat and support. The stress caused by radical changes in the culture, plus the clergy's lack of preparation for innovative leadership, makes the minister's task exceedingly difficult.

Second, when persons who have been out of church for a long time return seeking a vital faith, where will they find it? Many traditional church members do not know how to speak of their faith to an inquiring person. Yet, the small group can serve as a laboratory where seekers can be exposed to authentic faith.

Finally, the small group with its emphasis on shared leadership provides a setting for birthing a new kind of leader for the church. Through their immersion in sharing, fellowship, and discernment, persons who take root in these groups will be better equipped to free us from today's management mentality and to direct our attention to the voice of the Spirit.

Because small groups are personal, they can adapt to each person's personal needs. Ron Habermas, Christian education expert and professor of biblical studies at John Brown University, says, "Small groups force people to think about and articulate what they believe in a way not usually possible with sermons and traditional Sunday school lectures. They prompt dialogue and can bring a person to greater ownership of beliefs."[49]

These small groups require the involvement of the pastor. As lay leaders also become involved in small groups, the benefits blossom throughout the life of the church.

THESIS #58
The re-formation of the whole begins with the transformation
of the few — persons who are salt, light, and leaven.

The Christian principle of the few who transform the whole first appears in the ministry of Jesus. He chose twelve disciples that they should be "with him" (Mark 3:14). He formed them into a small group, demonstrated his message, taught them, and sent them out to share in the task of ministry. In the group he listened to them, corrected them, and imparted wisdom to them.

This group of twelve had the task of leavening Israel and then the entire Gentile world. The small group acts like leaven hidden in the flour – small, inconsequential, but powerful and transformative.

The presence of small groups does not signal the absence of strong churches, notes Robert Wuthnow, director of Princeton's Center for the Study of American Religion. Instead small groups and strong churches go hand-in-hand.[50]

The principle of transformation begins by selecting a few in a particular church (especially the officers), training them, delegating the task of ministry to them, supporting them, and celebrating their victories with them. These few who are transformed by the Spirit will become leaven in a congregation by modeling a joyous, faithful, liberated lifestyle.

Power does not always reside in the majority. A focused minority exerts more power than a diffused majority.

THESIS #59
Persons called to this adventure must agree to meet together regularly for an agreed upon length of time in an agreed upon place.

The discipleship group must not expect instant transformation. Growth and change take time. The time requirement explains our encouraging group members to make a solid commitment to such basics as regular attendance, punctuality, confidentiality and prayer.[51]

Jesus describes the struggles of discipleship in the parable of the sower. When some hear the call, they will be like the seed that fell on the path. The seed of the Kingdom will not take root in them. Soon the very thought of a disciplined life will be snatched away and forgotten.

Others will be like the seed that fell on "rocky ground." They hear the call, rejoice in it for a season, but when schedules become cramped, they choose other priorities. Their enthusiasm turns to disinterest.

Still others will receive the challenge, begin their time of meeting, and share their lives to a point. Then other concerns will challenge this new, intentional commitment. The search for money, pleasures, and the high cost of friendships will become too dear and the original challenge will be choked out.

But in spite of all those who do not follow through, some will. These persons bring good soil to the seed. They hear the challenge for renewal and outreach, join the movement, stick with the commitment through thick and thin, and eventually bear abundant fruit in the life of the congregation.

Some will bear fruit thirty-fold, others sixty-fold, and still others will bear one-hundred-fold. Those who multiply the life, the message, and the ministry so many times will abundantly reward the minister of God for his or her investments.

THESIS #60
The small community will begin with simple disciplines that constitute the community of Christ.

In recent years my denomination commissioned a man to go about the church calling it to new life and focus. He sometimes speaks of his task as participating in the act of "re-inventing the church."

His primary ministry has been the formation of small, intentional groups that embody the Spirit of Christ. To open themselves to this Spirit, group participants agree to six spiritual disciplines.

They agree to pray together. The members may not know much about prayer; they may not have previously prayed very much, but they meet together to bring their lives, the community, and the church into the presence of God.

This group also shares struggles and joys. Members voice the issues that plague them daily like family problems, problems on the job, effectiveness in the community, and the struggle to pay bills. All these needs become subjects of prayer.

The members commit to listen for the voice of God in scripture. Notice the purpose for reading scripture: "to listen for the voice of God," not to learn some new doctrine as was the habit of the Athenians. This Voice gives focus to the group. Roberta Hestenes writes, "The Bible tells us the story of God's mighty words and actions... To seek to know this story better, and discover our place in it, we study the Bible. And because this story is the tale of a people, a community of faith, we find it helpful to read with others – to study the Bible in groups."[52]

This group also seeks to discern its context. What is going on in the larger society? Where are the needs? Most often they look for the places of pain in society because Christian vocation bends toward pain.

Discernment does not stop short of action. The group responds to the call of God. Where is the Spirit of Christ at work? How can we join

Christ in what he is doing among the people in our ministry area?

Those who engage in ministry make themselves accountable to each other and to the larger church. No group, no matter how dedicated or passionate, can be allowed to forge ahead without discipline and direction.

Thesis #61
This disciplined group will intentionally reach out to others and include them in its communal life.

The very existence of an intentional group suggests the multiplication of its life. One group begets other groups. As groups multiply they will not only begin to "leaven" the whole church but they will be open to include persons who have not yet become associated with the church.

Whereas the Constantinian church often lacks the power to transform, these intentional, focused groups have that capability. Transformation does not derive from the power of the members but from the Christ who is part of their lives and who holds the community together.

So, the future outreach of congregations will center in these living cells. Persons who participate in them are changed by the fellowship in the Spirit. Their change releases enormous energy which finds expression in ministry.

Persons within the disciple's circle of influence will recognize the change that has occurred. They will inquire. Witness will follow. The witness will be accompanied by an invitation into the fellowship of the group. "Small groups offer a platform to build relationships that reach people for Christ," says Judy Hamlin.[53]

With new persons entering, the group becomes the training ground for new disciples as well as a place for discerning ministry. Any active imagination can conceive how such groups could multiply in communities and become the primary model of ministry for the future.

Thesis #62

This intentional community will provide the setting for personal transformation, leadership development, and equipping for mission and ministry.

Recovering a sense of God's presence, the shift from maintenance to mission, liberation of the laity, and the renewal of mainline congregations depend upon a spiritually transformed membership. This transformed body stands in contrast to the cultural church that makes no demands and exhibits no courage in confronting the challenges of the age.

Transformation cannot be accomplished by humans with a series of quick, easy-to-follow programs. Transformation depends upon the Spirit and the secret working of God's truth in the lives of women and men. This work of the Spirit often closely relates to the Word of God. As John Calvin explains, "God works in his elect in two ways: within, through his Spirit; without through the Word. By his Spirit, he makes them a new creation. By his Word, he arouses them to desire, to seek after, and to attain that same renewal."[54] Reading the text of scripture with openness and vulnerability about our own lives permits the Spirit to bring to mind both necessary changes and the promise of needed graces.

Persons with some first-hand experience of the Spirit will give leadership in Future Church. These will not be pious men and women who consider themselves experts, but persons who have a sense of "rightness," or the appropriate action to take or course to follow in a given situation. With this conviction about the presence of God comes courage to act in difficult times and places.

These ministers of God, both ordained and non-ordained, learn how to minister in the "give and take" of life around the Word of God and in the presence of the Spirit. They bring life issues into the light of the Word of God and in conversation with this community find answers to their questions. The practice of ministry – discerning the community and the call to engagement – provides experience in a setting of accountability and feedback.

The small, experimental community seems indispensable in calling forth Future Church. Many experts expect small groups to become the primary ministry of Future Church. "[Small groups] are not one program among many; they are the program through which all ministry is accomplished."[55]

THESIS #63
The future of the church depends upon leaders who have been birthed, formed, and nurtured in the environment of vital faith.

Participating in a small group provides many of the skills women and men need for effective leadership for the future. They mature in a personal relationship with Christ; they experience his presence in their midst. Through repeated exposure to him, their lives are gradually transformed into the same likeness "from one degree of glory to another" (2 Cor. 3:18).

In this community participants learn to listen to the Word of God in the context of their lives. Bible reading and study do not become ends in themselves but rather a means of coming to know God. The knowledge of God empowers and informs both life and ministry.

When a community of believing persons addresses a particular situation by the truth of God, discernment occurs. The proper course of action is determined through discerning both the context with its need and the text of Scripture with its revelation. The habit of discernment enables persons to ask, "What does God will?" instead of "What do I think we ought to do?"

Because groups are personal, each person can receive individual attention. "The key to person-centered ministry," writes Stanley Ott, "is to find aspects of Christian maturity that will allow each person to grow within his or her own limits and abilities. Oswald Chambers said, 'Allow the Holy Spirit the same freedom with the next person that He had with you.'"[56]

In the group, individuals discern their particular gifts, have them affirmed by fellow members of Christ's Body, and learn to use these gifts for the benefit of the whole community. Gifts released within the community empower it for God's larger ministry in the world.

Members of this spiritual community also learn to care for each other in struggles and failure. We are not always successful either in our intentions or actions. We need to know how to forgive, affirm, and be with persons who have failed.

Thesis #64

The selection, training, and support of the leaders for these small, intentional communities will be a primary task of ordained ministers.

In Future Church the mission will be conducted by well-equipped lay men and women who have a call and the gifts to fulfill it. Churches that rely on a volunteer ministry which primarily enlists the most available persons will need to change their approach. Instead of mere availability, the desirable criteria for lay ministers will be gifts, commitment, and a sense of God in their work.

The ordained minister must share in the selection of lay ministers. Other persons in the community and the concurrence of the individual constitute part of the call. In the whole process the lay minister knows him or herself to be set in the Body by God.

Calling requires training. "It is the pastor's first responsibility to train [lay leaders] in how to be effective, and it is [their] first responsibility to train the pastor in how to be an effective pastor."[57] Lay ministers need to know the history, tradition, and authoritative norms for making decisions. This training will be provided by the ordained minister, the practical theologian in the church.

Unlike the minister who "went away" for the three year monastic existence of seminary, lay persons must receive on-the-job training. In the give and take of life, in the struggle with the powers that control us today, these followers of Christ must live out their obedience.

This need for training challenges the clergy to engage lay men and women in unaccustomed ways. Experiment, trial-and-error, mutual discovery – these may be the forms through which mutual learning occurs. Clergy can be joint learners instead of authoritative instructors.

Thesis #65

The spiritual life and vision of a community of lay ministers provides vital respite, nurture, and support for weary pastors.

Who could better care for a pastor than the lay men and women with whom the pastor has shared ministry? This minister of God has lovingly entered into the suffering of lay persons, sharing their pain, confusion, and ambiguity. They know that she or he has been there for them when they desperately needed someone.

Who could be more motivated or equipped to minister to a pastor than those who have been nurtured by him or her? The bond already exists. The ground work for caring has been laid and those who have received ministry are eager to return it.

In the Body of Christ, "if one member suffers, all suffer together; if one member is honored, all rejoice together" (1 Cor. 12:26). No minister feels more rewarded than the one who equips members as caregivers, only to discover that the very care that was both taught and given is returned to the minister during times of need.

Ministers equipping laity to be the church need much more than a pat on the back and a glib word of a job well done. They need women and men of God who know how to be with them in dark hours, who believe in them and pray for them. Multiply these spiritually sensitive persons and the minister has enormous resources for facing changes, rejection, and pain.

PERSPECTIVE ON PASTORS

THESIS #66
Because of today's radical and abrupt cultural changes, clergy face dislocation and ever increasing stress.

In the days of Christendom clergy knew both their role and place. They were the officers of the church, the keepers of tradition, and the mediators between the community and God. Theirs was a place of recognition and honor. "Parson" meant the "person" in the community.

With the demise of Christendom these certainties and the clarity they brought have eroded. In place of honor and recognition today's minister of God becomes the target of jokes. Movies, sitcoms, and newscasts often stereotype the minister as a pompous hypocrite.

Many persons in the secular world see the minister as a self-centered manager of a religious institution who needs them to fill pews and pay bills. Thus, they approach the minister with skepticism and hesitancy.

In some parts of the nation the distrust has turned to disdain and even anger. People resent the special privileges ministers receive such as housing allowances, benefits for which they do not pay taxes, and income that is not reported (though it should be).

This change of environment threatens the social place of the clergy person. She or he cannot count on trust, respect, or an automatic role in the community. The loss of social influence is most keenly felt among mainline ministers. "The visionary autocrats of yesteryear who wielded great personal power have given way to mere anonymous managers."[58]

Because of these changes many ministers experience the stress of dislocation and ambivalence about their identity. Stress unrelieved leads to "burnout" in which the minister no longer feels connected to the calling, no longer has energy for the tasks at hand, and often sinks into the pit of doubt and despair. We cannot expect visionary leadership from clergy who struggle merely to survive.

Thesis #67
Most clergy have been prepared to pastor congregations that no longer exist.

Clergy from traditional, denominational seminaries have received training to maintain an institution. In years gone by the local church stood secure in the community and in the larger culture. Ministers were equipped to lead the church according to a particular discipline or book of order. They were taught Bible and theology as a foundation for preaching. They received clinical pastoral education to equip them to care for parishioners. In some instances they learned about management and finance.

In recent years when these ministers have arrived in their parishes, membership has shrunk, parishioners are aging, funds are low, and the young people have disappeared. Ministers have found the culture ignorant of their discipline and often hostile to their endeavors.

These ministers discover that they no longer have the task of managing a healthy church but of practicing ministry in a missionary environment. Nothing can be taken for granted any more – identity, role, or place in the community.

Now ministers must learn to function as missionaries, and this requires them to be proactive in witnessing to the gospel. For many this new environment challenges the foundations of their faith and demands of them a witness for which they feel unprepared.

This frustration rises due to the necessity of funding the upkeep of buildings no longer in use. Too much time and energy must go into maintenance instead of mission. It would often be easier for these ministers to begin at the beginning without the albatross of the institution hanging around their neck.

Yet a denomination's loss of prominence brings with it a new freedom, notes Robert Lynn: "No longer need we do everything. In this freedom we have the gift to be selective and partial, and not feel guilty. That is part of the gift of being on the margin."[59]

Thesis #68
Contextual changes have been so swift and pervasive that clergy have been unable to make the necessary adjustments.

In the last 40 years monumental changes have challenged every practice of ministry.

Consider today's information technology. We can receive, process, and transmit complex data electronically in seconds. Through the personal computer, thousands of individuals benefit from capabilities once reserved for large companies with mammoth computing machines. For example, a typical laptop computer handles much more data than the computing monsters of the past, and it also processes it faster.

We receive news from around the world instantly. The 1991 Persian Gulf War was the first in history to be fully orchestrated on television. Like information, people move faster and more frequently than ever before. A decline of jobs in agriculture and manufacturing resulted in large scale migrations. This, coupled with the development of air travel and highways, has made mobility the norm, not the exception.

Physical mobility encourages a mobility of beliefs. The growing presence of Vietnamese, Cambodians, Chinese, Haitians, Cubans, Hispanics, and Middle-Easterners in America means a wider spectrum of religious practice. "Increased travel by college students, business people, and tourists has served to widen our experience of the relativity of our lifestyles and values," notes developmental theorist James Fowler.[60]

With such mobility of place, information, and belief, many Americans no longer expect to keep the same job, the same hometown, or even the same faith tradition for life.

THESIS #69
Old models of ministry are inadequate for the present age.

Present day ministry has been characterized and informed by numerous models. These models have usually grown out of secular movements that found their way into the church. Often by the time the secular ideal has become passe the church still seeks to perpetuate it.

For example, some ministers see themselves as protectors of the tradition. In this model the minister seeks to preserve not only the values of the past but also the forms that were born in another era, whether those forms be liturgy, church structure, or statements of faith.

Other ministers have sought to be educators of the people. In this model, the minister becomes chief teacher of the people. Even sermons possess a didactic flavor and have the dullness of a lecture.

About the time widespread reliance on the educator model sank into oblivion, the therapist model appeared. Sermons, worship, pastoral care, and even classes took on a therapeutic tone. The mission of the church became the healing of the soul, understood in psycho-dynamic terms.

Then came the manager model. The business world proposed "management by objectives" and the church latched onto this detached way of being the People of God. Even renewalists touted the power of clearly stated goals and carefully developed strategies to reform the church. Alas, the MBO model has failed.

Although the context has changed, the call of ministry remains the same as that received by the Apostles. "The recovery of apostolic ministry of the clergy, and all the people of God, to peoples who do not yet believe is perhaps the most significant movement in the world Church in our lifetime,"[61] writes George G. Hunter.

THESIS #70
Clergy will probably find their greatest source of help in pondering the role and image of the minister of God set forth in the Old and New Testaments.

Scripture reveals the long history and unique calls of patriarchs, prophets, disciples and apostles, elders and deacons. Their encounters with God may provide the best material for reflecting upon the identity of the ordained minister.

When God called Moses, he felt his own inadequacy and lack of preparation to deliver the people. But none of his rationalizations changed God's mind. God chose Moses for the Deliverer!

When God elected David to lead the people, David did not realize he possessed gifts for this role. But God chose him to be the King of Israel, to unite the factions and to rule the nation.

God's encounters with the prophets provide yet another perspective. In the temple , for example, God spoke to Isaiah through smoke, fire, and quaking (Is. 6:1-8). Isaiah heard the voice asking, "Whom shall I send and who will go for us?"

Samuel had a divine intervention in his life. The Lord called his name: "Samuel..." He did not know the one who called nor the meaning of the voice. After several encounters, the High Priest, Eli, told Samuel to answer, "Speak Lord, your servant is listening!" (1 Sam. 3:9).

The image of Jesus in the New Testament offers more material as we imagine a new ministerial image. We are called to be "Christ-persons," "little Christs," "followers of the Way," and "Christian." As Jacques Ellul wrote, "In the sight of men and in the reality of this world, the Christian is a visible sign of the new covenant which God has made with this world in Jesus Christ."[62]

For Enlightenment ministers these models may seem far too religious, and that is precisely the attitude we must escape. We must no longer fear being identified with Jesus of Nazareth as his spokesperson, follower, minister, or servant.

What about the simple title, "Man of God," or "Woman of God"?

THESIS #71
An effective model of ministry flows out of and is accompanied by the minister's embrace of a serious spiritual journey.

If ministers are men and women of God, they must spend time with God to have this sense of identity verified by the Spirit. Time with God exposes them not only to the texts of sacred writings but also to themselves in the Divine Presence. In the encounter with God all of life comes under divine scrutiny.

Ministers who are not earnestly on their own journey become obvious to the congregation. They speak from memory, minister routinely, and lead worship as those who have lost touch with the original meaning of the faith. Others consider them professional Christians at best or phonies at worst. Imitation is difficult to hide.

By contrast, ministers who are intentionally on their journey reveal their intent by the way they pray, the way they preach, the way they encounter others, and the vision that dominates their ministry. Persons who come into contact with them recognize the vitality and depth of their faith.

Spiritually sensitive ministers take soberly their commitment to God, look at the events of their lives through faith, seek to discern what God is saying to them, and live with a sense of expectancy of the God who comes. Unlike many of their colleagues, they pray. They pray not only on Sundays when liturgy calls for them to pray; they pray daily, hourly, moment by moment for the assistance of the Spirit.

A life of prayer proves contagious. One pastor noticed that parishioners where hungry not "to get facts on the Philistines and Pharisees but to pray... Out of that recognition a conviction grew: that my primary educational task as a pastor was to teach people to pray."[63]

THESIS #72
As they journey with God, clergy will learn anew to speak of God in simple, personal, and experiential terms.

One of the blights on contemporary clergy manifests itself in our inability to speak of God in a simple, direct way. Clergy have been trained to speak in theological language but often the words they use have no experiential grounding. Frequently clergy talk in psychological verbiage, even casting the faith in terms of personal fulfillment or the therapeutic aspects of salvation. Other clergy have succumbed to ecclesiastical speech, which means little to them or to the persons with whom they minister.

Ministers who walk with God - who look for God in their darkness, in their joys, in the ambiguity of their daily lives, and in the helplessness of the marginalized - can speak. Their language about God has been squeezed out of their faith as it has rubbed against the joy and pain of persons inside the church and without.

Ministers who are seriously on their journey will become more familiar with the living God. Their prayer will acquaint them with the Sacred One. Their journey will give them access to their own story and a theological understanding of life. In their pastoral care they will pay attention to the stories of members and will help interpret them.

Television, writes George Hunter, has permanently altered the attention span of Americans. The most effective mode of communication is "animated dialogue." The minister must learn to speak of God on the sidewalk, not only in the pulpit.[64] These ministers will restore conversation about faith and life in the congregation.

THESIS #73
Effective clergy will claim their authority without becoming authoritarian.

Ministers of God receive ordination to confirm their authority as spokespersons for God, as administrators of the sacraments, and as theological voices in the community of faith. They have an identity as "Women" and "Men" of God.

The minister of God speaks for God in proclamation. No person controls the preacher of the gospel. When ministers read the text, open its meaning to the congregation, and bring it to bear upon questions of daily life, they speak in the place of God. Paul says, "We are spokespersons for Christ..." (2 Cor. 5:20)

In leading worship the minister speaks the word of forgiveness, God's absolving the people of their sins. When she has prayed the prayer of confession with the people, the minister can then say, "In the name of Jesus Christ you are forgiven." On behalf of Christ the minister announces the forgiveness of sin.

In teaching the people and in discerning the Spirit's guidance, the minister draws upon biblical, theological, and historical training. Without being dogmatic or dictatorial, the minister brings his or her understanding of scripture and the tradition to a decision. This gift enables the congregation to make faithful decisions, and it provides a source of authority from which the minister must not retreat.

In the storms of change congregations need clear, convinced voices of leadership. The malaise of the mainline church too often saps the confidence of mainline ministers. Yet the storms of change may be signs of beginnings, not endings. "Perhaps the British historian Paul Johnson will prove to be right in suggesting that the current crisis of the mainliners is actually the birth pangs of the Fourth Great Awakening," writes Leander Keck.[65] As we ministers exercise our God-appointed places of leadership in this time of change, the church will be stronger, more confident, and more focused in its mission.

THESIS #74
Secure pastors will liberate, welcome, equip, and support the lay apostolate.

Few would doubt that the church has been and continues to be clericalized. Whatever the form of government, clergy persons exercise a disproportional amount of influence.

Someone has pointed out that lawyers run the legal system; doctors run the medical system. In this arrangement others have little influence or power. The systems are closed, and "lay men and women" in the field have no voice. Sadly, this is also largely true with the church.

The many reasons for the clericalizing of the church do not need exposure here. The system has been inherited and exercises such strength that it will take a massive collapse to change it. In part the system serves clergy like the legal and medical systems serve lawyers and doctors. No small group of ministers can revamp the system any more than a small group of doctors can reverse the medical system.

Even though they may not change the system, secure, mature clergy who recognize the energy that comes from a liberated laity will relinquish false power for the laity's sake. Conversely, "pastors that have a need to be needed in order to find validation for their ministry will have a hard time giving up control of the actual ministry to the congregation."[66] Visionary ministers recognize that a local congregation can be transformed through the involvement of a cadre of committed and equipped laity.

Thesis #75
Ministers of God must resist the temptation to alleviate their stress through immoral sexual liaisons, drugs, alcohol, or the consumption of goods and pleasure.

Change. Demands. Anxiety about place and future. Troubled marriages. Children that betray the faith. Such things plague men and women of God who minister in pulpits large or small. More stress falls upon the minister than he or she can handle.

Because of the stress, ministers today find themselves in untenable and unacceptable practices. Some ministers in their loneliness find release in the arms of a "lover" who offers words of appreciation and comfort. Pastoral counseling can heighten the risk of illicit liaisons as desirable emotions of care and compassion easily lead to undesirable emotions of sexual attraction.[67] Sexual affairs have multiplied in recent years.

If not to a sexual liaison, the minister may turn to alcohol for relief. The occasional, social drink turns into two or three or six, and before anyone realizes the power of the habit, the minister has become an alcoholic. Following hard on the heels of this aberration in character comes the necessity to hide, make excuses, and deny the fact until the evidence becomes so great that the minister collapses and the congregation suffers a loss of faith.

Is this kind of behavior in any way related to the loss of faith that clergy have suffered? Or, to their disillusionment with the parish? Or, to the lack of a profound sense of God in their lives?

THESIS #76

Above all, clergy who are pioneering a new day for the church will not retreat from the struggle to equip the new church to meet the challenges forced upon it.

The temptation to fall back never leaves us! Always there are two ways before us: the way of pursuing a career and the way of dangerous obedience. Ministers who have a primary commitment to their own advancement and career will say the acceptable word, compromise their convictions, and go to great lengths to be well-liked and popular. At times they convince themselves that these choices are really for the good of the church and come from holy motives. In moments of nakedness in the Presence they know better.

The other pathway calls for hard obedience. It costs us to speak the truth in love, to create boundaries, to take a stand for what is right! Theology matters to a minister of God. "Our 'hermeneutic of suspicion' must be balanced by one of affirmation," notes Leander Keck. "The hermeneutic of affirmation is a persistent but pained loyalty to a heritage, which, though flawed, nonetheless has given us what faith we have and which is supple enough to survive what we will do to it."[68]

At no time in recent decades has the church faced such high stakes: faithful witness, secular oppression, popular derision, economic pressure, and threatened survival. The old ways are not working! New ways have not yet been born. The people of God find themselves caught between the "changing of the times." It is frightening, painful, and confusing.

But this also represents one of the greatest opportunities the church has faced in recent history! The church has a chance to recover from the staid, ineffective forms of the past. It can be born anew!

The opportunity before us challenges faithful ministers to commit themselves to the future, to equip the congregation to imagine its life in new ways, and to follow with faith the path of risky obedience.

THESIS #77

Women and men have an equal partnership in the transformation of the ministry of Christ.

Why has God called so many women into ordained ministry in the past twenty years? From the mid-70s to the mid-80s, the number of ordained women in U.S. churches doubled, with most of the increase occurring in mainstream Protestantism.[69] Many of these women exhibit manifold gifts for the leadership, nurture, and renewal of congregations.

Is the answer to be found in the feminist revolution? Does the opening of ordained ministry to women solve the issue? Is this some sort of "dispensation" of the woman? Or have women simply listened to God's call with more sensitive ears?

Why did this phenomenon erupt in the church at the close of the century? Maybe the question lacks legitimacy. Yet, it seems a fair question. What is God saying to the church through the "other" gender?

Too often women's experience has not been valued as a resource for the church. Carol Ochs in her book *Women and Spirituality* defines spirituality as "de-centering the self" or "dying to the self," which is precisely what motherhood involves. This is just one example of the spiritual resources in women which the church has overlooked.[70]

Without falsely glorifying women in ministry, we must recognize that the white, male-dominated church of the West is disappearing. Women will make a difference in the heart and form of Future Church!

So we males will welcome women into the constructive enterprise of recreating the church – not the essence of the church, but its form. Women's voices, their intuitions, and their visions will be a counter-point to the hard-driving, military-like church of the past. Women will help the people of God recover an appropriate spirituality, a receptivity to the stranger, and a passion for service to the margins that has often been lacking among us.

Women and men will learn to welcome one another into this creative endeavor and together we will find the right pathway into the future!

PERSPECTIVE ON THE SEMINARIES

THESIS #78
The relevant seminary will radically alter its vision, curriculum, and priorities to prepare ministers for their tasks in the emerging world.

Seminaries, in contrast to divinity schools, owe their first loyalty to the church. They have their origin in the church; they receive their support from the church; and they primarily exist to equip ministers for leadership in the church.

These professional "offspring" of the church often become divided between the academic guild and the church. Some professors look to the guild for their affirmation and fulfillment rather than to the church that funds the seminary.

With this conflict between commitments, denominational seminaries struggle to clarify a vision for their task. On the one hand, scholars wish to make their mark in the academic world. On the other hand, they desire to prepare ministers for effective ministry in the church. Seeking to keep the proper balance often creates a problem.

The curriculum often encourages academic prowess while neglecting church-oriented leadership. As a result students learn the latest theories on the "Historical Jesus" but do not know how to utilize this information when they pastor congregations.

"Seminaries share with other professional schools a dual responsibility: Training for the profession and scholarship relevant to that training purpose. Under optimum conditions there is a healthy tension between the two."[71]

The priority of seminaries should be to serve the church. There are enough divinity schools for students desiring an academic career. The church needs more schools committed to preparing pastors.

THESIS #79

The forward-looking seminary will shift from a maintenance to a missional program of training, recognizing that it is equipping missionaries to work in a culture alien to the gospel.

Unquestionably, seminaries intend to prepare leaders for the church. Yet too many seminaries still prepare ministers to maintain institutional churches in a culture that has radically changed. The effective pastor in the twenty-first century will be a missionary in an alien culture.

God calls the church to make disciples of Jesus Christ. No longer can this task be accomplished merely by baptizing the children of members. With an aging membership and a generation that has not returned to the church, the church will have fewer and fewer children to baptize.

The minister of the twenty-first century will lead a missionary endeavor in a pagan culture. The task facing this generation of ministers will be very much like that of the first century church. As in the Apostle Paul's day, the church will be surrounded by pagans who believe that one religion is as good as another. Churches will not receive support from the government nor the culture. The people Christians encounter will know nothing about the faith, so instruction must begin at the beginning. This new situation, while appearing tragic and depressive, actually provides a great opportunity.

THESIS #80

Both seminary curriculum and the style of teaching should be informed by the shifts in the culture and the gifts candidates bring to their training.

The medium is the message! Therefore, *how* seminary professors teach students commands as much importance as what they teach. The new situation demands a different approach to teaching.

Seminary training must take into account that many who seek training for ministry cannot leave a job, family, or security to retreat to an institution for three years. In "Seminaries: Back to the Future," Wilson Yates pronounces the old stereotyped seminarian dead. "This hovering specter is a white, unmarried, heterosexual male, roughly 24 years old, adherent to his denominational tradition from the cradle, a graduate of a good liberal arts college, and preparing for the ordained ministry."[72]

Today's different student body brings new needs. Seminaries must discover and employ ways to provide "distance learning" for seminarians. In addition to distance learning through satellite schools, seminaries today will do well to investigate the capability of "on-line" learning through computer networks.

Already, the growing access to on-line libraries is quickly making brick-and-mortar libraries obsolete. The on-line information publicly available in the late twentieth century represents just three percent of what we will have at our fingertips in 2010.[73] Seminaries must explore the computer's potential for providing instruction, supervision, and resources to "distance learners."

Today's student body contains many "second career" persons and a high percentage of women. Effective education should take into account that many seminary students have years of experience in the church. Others have worked in secular vocations and developed skills that could be shared with fellow seminarians. When seminaries disregard such skills, they bypass a great resource and offend gifted students in the process.

Since women now compose forty to fifty percent of many seminary student bodies, the style and content of instruction should take into account the differences in learning, gifts, and leadership styles. These changes will be part of genuine renewal in seminaries.

Thesis #81
Seminaries should be as committed to excellence in spiritual formation for future ministers as they are to excellence in academic preparation.

Accredited theological institutions have traditionally succeeded in providing good academic training for future ministers of the church. The fields of practical theology, Bible, church history, and theology have been adequately covered, orienting the minister to the tradition and practice of ministry. Scholarship has varied from acceptable to excellent.

Without question, the academic dimension of theological training cannot be compromised. To compromise the academic element results in soft thinking, fundamental ignorance, and poor preparation for effective ministry. Sound scholarship must continue without interruption.

On the other hand, many academics assume that if these disciplines are given proper attention, spiritual formation will take care of itself. Indeed, enormous energy is exerted to keep the present model of education intact.

In earlier years, theological seminaries understood their primary task as shaping men and women to be servants of Christ in the church. In the intervening years this aspect of preparation has been neglected to the impoverishment of ministers and the dismay of the laity whom they pastor.

For the sake of Future Church, theological seminaries must once again embrace the task of shaping ministers spiritually as well as intellectually. The new challenges of missionary ministry in America will elevate prayer, discipleship, and discipline to a new place of importance in theological education.

Thesis #82
The seminary community should conduct its life in a manner that models Future Church.

Life together and models of instruction either prepare or inhibit effective ministry in the churches. Too often, in their effort to prepare ministers, seminaries perpetuate a campus community that is academic, instructional, and competitive. Henri Nouwen writes, "It is obvious that in a system that encourages this ongoing competition, knowledge no longer is a gift that should be shared, but a property that should be defended."[74] Yet if life in the seminary community bears no resemblance to life in the community of faith, the shock of adjustment for the newly ordained minister becomes severe.

Again, the models of instruction in the seminary tend toward lecture. Often, it represents a unilateral process: the professor knows and the student learns. Certainly the professor should be free to instruct, but the implied hierarchy models a superior/inferior relationship that easily translates into the pastor who knows and the laity who must learn from the pastor.

If these traditional models were transformed, students and professors would interact with openness to God and each other. In the community, students would experience professors as vulnerable, struggling human beings as well as scholars and intellectual giants. The mystique would then dissolve and these fellow members of the Body of Christ would find each other mutually instructive and supportive. Their connection in Christ should take away fear of the professor and increase trust in the students.

Students trained in a community of faith in collegiality with professors and administrators would learn to work in the church as leaders who relate with laity both as teachers and learners. In this kind of bilateral learning, "it is not so much the intellectual superiority of the teacher that counts as it is his/her maturity in facing the unknown and his/her willingness to leave unanswerable questions unanswered."[75] Such a transformation in theological education is imaginable and possible.

THESIS #83
Seminaries will be called to fill a new role as a result of the demise of national denominational bureaucracies.

 Many persons aware of present circumstances doubt that national denominational agencies will continue to exist in any meaningful way. These agencies reflect a bureaucratic form fueled by the uncritical embrace of the latest secular techniques.

Several factors feed this judgment. First, national agencies have delivered ineffective programs and materials to local congregations. Much of the problem stems from an effort to create acceptable programs for religiously and culturally diverse congregations. This all-encompassing aim had no bite or persuasive power!

In many instances congregations suspect national agencies care more about themselves than local churches. "Just as any hierarchical and tightly organized managerial enterprise will build alienation, alienation grew to a sort of fruition in the churches in the cultural upheavals beginning in the 1960s."[76] Even those good programs conceived by denominational leaders will soon be defunct due to a lack of financial support. When the funds run out, the work will stop.

The demise of national agencies will not spell disaster. Congregations existed, often with a high degree of health, before program agencies came into being. They will continue to exist and function with effectiveness. Note, for example, the degree of effectiveness of non-denominational churches that have no bureaucratic structure.

As agencies of the denomination cease to provide programs, training, and support, a greater burden will fall on the seminary and teaching churches. Pastors and lay persons will look to theological institutions to fill the gap vacated by the agencies of the denomination.

THESIS #84
Theological seminaries will fulfill their mission only as they become servants of the church and respond to new demands placed upon them.

Theological seminaries have the capability to provide leadership to a church in crisis. In some sense the seminary should represent the "brain trust" of the church. This does not mean to establish the superiority of professors over practitioners, but it points to the vocation of scholars. Seminaries should responsibly communicate their knowledge throughout the church.

Given this thesis, however, seminaries must have twin foci: training future ministers for the church and supporting ministers and laity within the church. Most seminaries have a long-standing, clear commitment to the first task.

But, too often, the seminary does not recognize its growing role in providing support for persons already serving in churches. When administrators and faculty come to grips with this new reality, it will call for more attention to the continued work of equipping and it will force seminary leaders to re-think the role and form of theological education.

Theological extension centers will multiply during the next decade and should now be a priority in the plans of denominational seminaries. New ways of providing theological training will also make use of the appropriate technology - for example, the technology already available for electronic instruction, using a camera/phone/keyboard combination with students around the globe. Lectures can be delivered and assignments received through the two-way system.[77] The Middle Ages delivery systems – chalkboards, paper, and ink – are not adequate for providing training, nurture, and support in Future Church. The time to launch change for the future is now!

THESIS #85
Any seminary curriculum that does not aim at preparing ministers for effective ministry in a changed church in a changing world is irrelevant.

The changes that have befallen the church have shifted its place in the society. The North American church of the twenty-first century will be a missionary church. The context in which it does ministry will become increasingly hostile and its place of privilege will be eroded by secular values.

Most curricula of denominational seminaries prepare ministers to manage institutions that cannot continue to exist in their present form. Examine the curriculum of any denominational seminary and discover that the bulk of required courses still concentrates in theology, history, and Bible. Pastoral courses tend to assume that the future will be an extension of the past.

New curriculum must assume that the church will minister in a missionary situation in which most persons do not have the rudiments of faith. Evangelism will no longer be the enlistment of new members without proper instruction. Church growth will not be the addition of names to the role to preserve the institution. The basic work of teaching and witnessing to the faith of Christ must be done.

The seminary that endures will equip ministers to be missionaries in an alien culture. Mission work requires a high degree of commitment. Often the missionary has few resources with which to work. Creativity, innovation, and imagination provide the keys to a missionary's survival. Since the church as an institution no longer receives automatic authority, it will reclaim respect through relevance, not through dictating. In a missionary situation, "we can gain people's confidence not by raving about pure spiritual truths, but about truth as it relates to people's daily struggles."[78]

A seminary that moves in this direction will not only "serve the present age" but it will serve the Ages! Ministers will encourage prospective students to attend this kind of forward–looking school.

THESIS #86
Teachers and leaders in the seminary are called to confess their sins as participants in the creation and support of Future Church.

Repentance precedes change! The present church, so ill–equipped for the future, exists in part because of the theological vision carried in the hearts of clergy. One does not wish to criticize them severely. They are producing what their role models showed them.

Repentance means an honest appraisal of the situation, the acceptance of responsibility, and appropriate change. We have been faithful to an old paradigm no longer appropriate for the mission of the church.

To prepare ministers for missionary service in a pagan American culture, theological leaders of the church must rethink their present formulations of truth, their manner of teaching, and their role in supporting tomorrow's clergy. When these issues are placed at the center of the faculty table, new energy will be released in the seminary community and in the lives of seminary students. This shift will give birth to new leadership in the church.

How can the chief proponents of change in the church refuse to change themselves?

PERSPECTIVE ON THE DENOMINATION

THESIS #87
Mainline churches as we have known them for the past century are in disarray and decline, facing death.

This situation grows steadily worse and yet leaders of these denominations seem unable to stop the gradual demise. When a denomination consistently loses 40,000 members each year, it races toward the time when it will have no more members to lose. This hard fact alone should shock national and local leadership into realizing that the present strategy for the church is not working.

The median age in these declining congregations is about 55 years. More members die each year than are being brought into the church. The loss of this older generation creates further complications.

As membership has declined in recent decades, the older generation has shouldered the burden of ministry. Indeed, the decline of mainline denominations may be traced to the "Baby Boomer" generation's preoccupation with self-fulfillment and disillusionment with the major institutions in society - including the church. "The fact is that the more strongly one holds to an ethic of self-fulfillment, the less likely one is to belong to the church."[79]

Those Baby Boomers who return to the church do not have the same stewardship habits of their parents. They do not give sacrificially! In thirty years the "giving" generation will be dead and the church will be without these funds except for endowment.

When a denomination closes and merges more churches than it spins off or develops, soon that denomination will no longer exist. The priority of mainline churches has shifted from building churches and reaching unchurched persons to other areas of important ministry. But to move into the future with life and energy will require that we give renewed priority to new church development.

Let no one claim, "We are reducing the ranks to strengthen the mission." The mission is not stronger but weaker. This rationalization has burned out, and most serious people see it as a gross misrepresentation.

Thesis #88

The loss of members, the loss of influence, the loss of established place in the society, and the unwillingness to face the reasons for these losses herald our demise.

The real reason for decline must be found in our unwillingness to be the church - our loss of grounding. When the content of our faith makes no demands, the whole enterprise of faith becomes trivialized.

Once again the church must struggle with its earliest creed: Jesus Christ is Lord! The person of Jesus Christ provides the most critical issue facing the church today. Jesus Christ is the foundation of the church; he is the life of the church; he is the Lord of the church and will lead it into the future.

Leander Keck notes that theological clarity proves essential for church renewal. "Today, theology – broadly understood – is like a state fair without a midway: Everything is going on at the same time and there is no main exhibit... Can anyone deny that the theological climate is a factor in the decline and shrinkage of the mainline churches?"[80]

"Jesus is Lord" affirms that he is more than a Hebrew prophet who became aware of the Spirit and drank more deeply than others. He is neither a revolutionary Zealot leading an insurrection against the Roman occupation, nor a mere Essene with a disciplined life and an expectation of the Son of Man from heaven, nor a Gnostic preaching rejection of the flesh and cultivation of secret knowledge.

Jesus is the Son of God. When Jesus asked the disciples who he was, Peter quickly replied, "You are the Christ, the Son of the Living God" (Matt. 16:16). Upon this confession he promised to build his church. And, the gates of Hades will not prevail against this church, but any other foundation will erode like sand. Persons who believe in the church, who take seriously the gospel, and who give their lives to this purpose of God believe Jesus Christ to be the central reality of the church.

Without the conviction that the Creator God is uniquely revealed in Jesus, the church wastes away. In a pluralistic age when many persons claim that personal opinions warrant as much merit as the long witness of the church, that one religion seems as good as another, and that all faith leads to the same God, the identity of Jesus Christ becomes a critical issue for the church.

The church dares to confess that Jesus Christ serves not only as the foundation of the church but also the clue that gives meaning to all human history. When we confess, "Christ has died, Christ has risen, Christ will come again," we speak of realities that shape the destiny of all creation, not just Christians.[81]

The church has believed for nearly twenty centuries that Jesus is one with God; that those who have seen him, have seen the Father; that Jesus is the way, the truth, and the life. There can be no good reason to give up these core Christian convictions.

THESIS #89
A disproportionate number of congregations are in conflict with themselves, their ministers, and the national church.

Recent reports indicate that the church exists in conflict. The reasons for this conflict are numerous. Many laity experience frustration because the old ways no longer work: the youth program has no youth, worship attendance declines, and the congregation ages, seemingly unable to attract new, young couples.

These congregations call a new pastor and expect him or her to fix the situation. When that does not occur, frustration turns into anger, conflict, and division. In serious conflict the church becomes preoccupied with itself and the mission of Christ suffers. Sharp divisions diminish the limited energy of a congregation, and feelings of alienation convince some people to leave the church.

In part the conflict arises from internal factors in the congregation – between pastor and people, between age-old factions. But instead of being resolved, these internal conflicts often express themselves as anger with the decisions of the national church. Geographic and relational distance between the local church and the national headquarters make it easier to express anger. Sometimes this anger is aimed toward a nameless, faceless bureaucracy and at other times toward the actions of unknown leaders.

Whatever the source of this widespread congregational conflict, the energy expended on fighting, posturing, and forming alliances undercuts the mission of the church and becomes a source of embarrassment. The church of the future must focus its concerns on the real enemy and stop killing off its own kin.

THESIS #90
*The national church has falsely envisioned itself as the true
and faithful church hampered by the lagging vision of
congregations.*

A larger perspective gives birth to a broader vision. Many who serve on the national church staff have the opportunity to view the Spirit's work in many parts of the nation and world. They recognize effective mission in a variety of situations.

Often, national staff members have information about the church's ministry unavailable to members of local congregations. And, many of these staff members converse about issues facing the church and form a consensus. Without the corrective of a congregation, the accountability of a session, and the hard realities of parish life and leadership, they make their decisions. Often their informed, closed, and idealistic judgments on current issues reach far beyond most congregations' capacity to affirm.

When these judgments have not been hammered out in the give-and-take of congregational life, the decisions and posturing of national staffs contradict the values and commitments of local churches. Conflict follows. In the wake of negative reactions, national staff members face criticism, hasty words of condemnation by local church members, and often threats of losing their jobs.

Due to this conflict, misunderstanding, and sometimes-stubborn persistence down a dead-end path, national staff feel alienated. Many staff members conclude that the local congregation only intends to conserve the past and resist all efforts to move into the future.

Lay people ask about the national staff: "Do they get it? ...That we are the Church of Jesus Christ and not just a consortium of political interests."[82]

This attitude of being "right" and "knowing" what the church should do crystallizes into the conviction that "we" have the truth and if the whole church would follow our lead, the church would be more effective and faithful. Attitudes that become crystallized then lead to an "us-versus-them" perspective. Nothing but fear, suspicion, and misunderstanding can result from this posture.

THESIS #91
The national church has for the most part lost touch with the "grass roots."

We all see the world from the place where we stand!

If the national staff of a denomination falls into the trap of viewing congregations as "the enemy" and itself as the "prophetic voice" with clear vision and undistorted truth, the local church member feels alienated and abused. In reality, local churches with their members cause the national bureaucracy to survive, not the other way around. "In the midst of denominational decline, congregational decline is truly the gravest danger we face."[83]

The church does not exist in bureaucracy but in congregations. Certainly those staff persons are not excluded from the church, but they are part of the church because they participate in congregations and worship with the people of God. They need congregations for their spiritual life as well as their vocational life.

Staff members of denominational agencies will make greater progress when they regard themselves as servants of the church and not its prophets or social critics. Harsh judgments, biting criticism, and questionable positions occur through a lack of accountability.

The future of most denominations might be brighter if all national staff were released and the process of re-imagining denominational needs, connections, and options was begun without interference from existing power brokers.

THESIS #92
The national church has lost credibility with many pastors, local congregations, and judicatories.

Because the leadership of the national church often takes positions in conflict with the values, vision, and commitments of local church members, this leadership does not represent the larger church. When members hear reports of the words and actions of national leaders that contradict their values, they no longer trust them. This distrust surfaces not only in withheld funds, but in giving designated for specific uses. "The selective participation in denominational life makes it difficult for denominational agencies to function, and raises profound questions about their future."[84]

When the denomination's highest governing body takes an action and the national staff begins immediately to undermine it, how can there be confidence? For example, the ruling body votes to reapportion the budget of the denomination so that $15 million will be set aside for the work of evangelism over a five year period. Because this shift would reapportion the denomination's allocations for mission, it sends shock waves through the national staff. The staff immediately goes to work undermining the action of the ruling body by "re-interpreting" the ruling.

The result: only one of the five proposed allocations for evangelism takes place while national leaders maneuver in the background to avoid following the intent of the ruling body's action. When such moves are repeated by the bureaucracy, how can the general membership of the church have confidence in its leadership?

To whom is a national staff subject? What accountability does it have to those who fund its very existence? The church has been dragged from the top for too long and the day has dawned for the push to come from below.

THESIS #93
The national church will continue to experience diminishing funds.

Income for denominational leadership will continue to decline for many reasons. First, income will diminish as congregations shrink. If the church continues to lose members, the base of giving will become smaller. For only so long can we expect more giving from fewer and fewer people.

In my own denomination, the Presbyterian Church (U.S.A.), national staffs recently underwent a significant downsizing. The denominational mission budget was underfunded by more than $2 million... [85]

The median age of members in most mainline denominations is about fifty-five. In thirty years most of the faithful, disciplined givers will be dead. The church is not replacing these members with committed disciples of Jesus Christ.

The generation born after the 1950s lacks the vision of its faithful parents. Though their parents may have supported the church and its missions, members of this generation do not have a loyalty to the institution and their tendency toward self-indulgence has led them to oppose sacrificial giving.

Conflict over policy, funding, and priorities will decrease the amounts of money given for denominational causes through national channels. Increasingly gifts will be designated and parachurch groups will receive a larger portion of congregational benevolences.

Loss of confidence from conflict over denominational policies, priorities, and behavior will inhibit generous funding from congregations.

Unless and until the national church works to regain the trust of its "grass roots" employers, congregational funding will decrease and this will eventually force a restructuring of top-heavy bureaucracies.

THESIS #94
The future mainline denomination cannot be birthed by the present bureaucratic leadership.

The loss of confidence, lack of vision, the effort to make every action acceptable to the broadest possible constituency, and the lack of entrepreneurship make the national leaders ill–equipped to lead the church into a new future.

This "new birth" of the church will not be directed by national bureaucracies, yet they are unlikely to sacrificially vote themselves out of existence. The governing body that created and controls these agencies lacks the vision or the courage to do away with antiquated forms of leadership.

John Mulder, president of Louisville Presbyterian Theological Seminary, suggests that mainline churches stop studying unhealthy churches and pay attention to thriving churches. "The next wave ... might look not at why this patient is sick, but why other patients are staying well."[86]

In a period of chaos the safety of the known seems better than the danger of daring actions, especially when the outcome remains uncertain. So, denominations will continue to invest money in a system that does not work because no matter how ineffective, it is familiar. Only when the money runs out will the existing structures be changed.

THESIS #95
New and living congregations with visionary pastors will give birth to new structures and appropriate judicatories for the church of the future.

A new vision for the denomination will not arise from the top but from the bottom. As congregations begin to show sparks of new life and as this new life spreads to other members, they will gain insight for the future. They will ask what this new life implies for the governance of the congregation and the denomination. They will find simple, workable, and less expensive ways to fulfill their obedience in the local congregation and beyond.

Laity often have less fear of change than ministers seeking to preserve career security and status. As one church member noted, "The church is the only community or organization to which I belong precisely in order to be disturbed."[87]

As "new vision" congregations begin to be established, they will find each other. Rays of light and bits of vision will be fused with those of other congregations. A new grass-roots connectionalism will emerge that will redefine structures for mission and accountability.

This emerging consensus will form itself into a coalition whose bonds will be stronger than any legislation can create. Shared faith, shared vision, shared action, and shared accountability will be at the heart of this new bonding of the Body of Christ.

The source of our creative vision and imagination derives from no human source but from God. "Our help is in the name of the Lord who made heaven and earth" (Psalm 121:2).

HOPE FOR THE FUTURE

"My hope is built on nothing less than Jesus' blood and right-eousness!" The gift of the Spirit leads us into an alternative future. We are not capable of creating the life of the Spirit in congregations nor of finding our way into the future. We are blinded by darkness, but Christ is the Light of the World. We do not know how to make our way into this alternative future, but Christ is the Way, the Truth and the Life. We do not know how to change, but he is salt, light, and leaven.

The birth of numerous dynamic communities of dedicated men and women will become the ferment for Future Church. These centers of renewal in every congregation will be receptors of the Spirit; they will be the center of discernment; and, they will spread like salt, light, and leaven.

A fellowship of daring, dedicated pastors will emerge who are willing to follow the lead of the Spirit without fear. Even the most dedicated cannot walk alone. The potential for self-destruction or self-delusion lurks so near that pastors dare not try going it alone. Men and women of vision need each other; they cannot make it into the future without com-panionship. But when vision joins vision, and courage charges courage, and our arms unite in trust and love, what we cannot do alone, we can do together.

Networks of renewed congregations will form the foundation or a new form of ministry together. They will begin to envision the shape of ture life together. Partial models of Future Church are already emerging. These congregations embrace change; they open themselves to the Spirit; they venture out into unexplored territories, and they find the pathway secure because Someone goes before them!

May the Day dawn and the Morning Star soon arise!

NOTES

1   Lesslie Newbigin, *The Gospel in a Pluralist Society* (Grand Rapids, MI: William B. Eerdmanns, 1989), pp. 143-144.

2   Leith Anderson, *Dying for Change* (Minneapolis: Bethany House, 1994), p. 15.

3   Milton J. Coalter, John M. Mulder, Louis B. Weeks, eds., *The Re-Forming Tradition: Presbyterians and Mainstream Protestantism,* 1st ed. (Notre Dame: University of Notre Dame Press, 1992), pp. 39-40

4   Tex Sample, *U.S. Lifestyles and Mainline Churches* (Louisville, KY: John Knox Press, 1990), p. 17.

5   George Barna, *The Barna Report: What Americans Believe* (Ventura, CA: Regal Books, 1991), p. 186.

6   Robert Bellah, *Habits of the Heart* (Berkeley, CA: University of California Press, 1991), p. 221.

7   Parker Palmer, *To Know As We Are Known* (San Francisco: Harper Collins, 1983), p. 10.

8   Leith Anderson, *Dying for Change* , p. 85.

9   Lesslie Newbigin, *The Gospel in a Pluralist Society*, p. 16.

10   Ibid, p. 103.

11   Loren Mead, *The Once and Future Church* (Washington, D.C.: The Alban Institute, 1991), p. 27.

12   William Easum, *Dancing with Dinosaurs* (Nashville: Abingdon Press, 1993), p. 14.

13   From James Hudnut Beumler's conference address *"Alternative Futures for American Mainline Protestant National Church Bodies"* at the Consultation on the Future of the Mainline Churches, sponsored by eleven mainline denominations, September 22, 1994, at Lisle, IL.

14   Presbyterian Survey, 1987.

15   Maria Harris, *Fashion Me a People* (Louisville, KY: Westminster/John Knox Press, 1989), p. 34.

16   Eugene Peterson, *The Contemplative Pastor* (Dallas: Word Publishing, 1989), p. 57.

17   Ibid, pp. 51-52.

18   Carol E. Becker in *Leading the Congregation* by Norman Shawchuck and Roger Heuser (Nashville: Abingdon Press, 1989), p. 255.

19   Kenneth R. Mitchell, *Multiple Staff Ministries* (Philadelphia: Westminster Press, 1988), p. 33.

20   Directory for Worship, W-1.3011, Presbyterian Church (U.S.A.).

21   Jurgen Moltmann, *The Church in the Power of the Spirit* (Philadelphia: Fortress Press, 1993), p. 197.

22   Kenneth R. Mitchell, *Multiple Staff Ministries*, p. 38.

23   Erich Lindemann, "Symptomatology and Management of Acute Grief," *The American Journal of Psychiatry 101*, September 1984.

24   Carol Becker in *Leading the Congregation* by Norman Shawchuck and Roger Heuser, p. 225.

25   John Leith, *Generation to Generation: the renewal of the church according to its own theology and practice* (Louisville, KY: Westminster/John Knox Press, 1990), p. 27.

26   E. Stanley Ott, *The Vibrant Church* (Ventura, CA: Regal Books, 1989), p. 10.

27   Ibid, p. 17.

28   Shirley Guthrie, *Christian Doctrine* (Atlanta: John Knox Press, 1968), p. 73.

29   George G. Hunter III, *How to Reach Secular People* (Nashville: Abingdon Press, 1992), p. 92.

30   William Easum, *Dancing with Dinosaurs* , p. 47.

31   James F. White, *Introduction to Christian Worship* (Nashville: Abingdon Press, 1992), p. 32.

32   Fred Craddock, *Preaching* (Nashville: Abingdon Press, 1985), p. 198.

33   Eugene Peterson, *The Contemplative Pastor*, p. 122.

34   William Easum, *Dancing with Dinosaurs*, p. 87.

35   Paul Hoon, *The Integrity of Christian Worship* (Nashville: Abingdon Press, 1971), p. 77.

36   George G. Hunter III, *How to Reach Secular People*, p. 147.

37   Dolores Leckey, *Laity Stirring the Church* (Philadelphia: Fortress Press, 1987), p. 102.

38   George Barna, *The Frog in the Kettle* (Ventura, CA: Regal Books, 1990), p. 117.

39   John Calvin, *Institutes, Book II*, Ch. XV, Section 5.

40   Leith Anderson, *A Church for the 21st Century* (Minneapolis: Bethany House, 1992), p. 132.

41   Jacques Ellul, *The Presence of the Kingdom* (Colorado Springs, CO: Helmers & Howard, 1989), p. 7.

42   William Easum, *Dancing with Dinosaurs*, p. 77.

43   Jurgen Moltmann, *The Church in the Power of the Spirit*, p. 24.

44   C. Ellis Nelson, *Helping Teenagers Grow Morally* (Louisville, KY: Westminster, 1992), p. 9.

45   David Bosch, *Transforming Mission* (Maryknoll, NY: Orbis Books, 1993), p. 117.

46   Roberta Bondi, *To Pray and To Love: Conversations on Prayer with the Early Church* (Minneapolis: Fortress Press, 1991), p. 105.

47   Norman Shawchuck and Roger Heuser, *Leading the Congregation* (Nashville: Abingdon Press, 1993), p. 206.

48   Maria Harris, *Fashion Me A People*, p. 29.

49   Ron Habermas quoted by Warren Bird, "The Great Small Group Takeover," *Christianity Today*, February 7, 1994, vol. 38, p. 29.

50   Robert Wuthnow, "How Small Groups are Transforming Our Lives," in *Christianity Today*, February 7, 1994, vol. 38, p. 23.

51   E. Stanley Ott, *The Vibrant Church*, p. 145.

52   Roberta Hestenes, *Using the Bible in Groups* (Philadelphia: Westminster Press, 1983), p. 9.

53   Judy Hamlin quoted by Warren Bird, "The Great Small Group Takeover," *Christianity Today*, February 7, 1994, vol. 38, p. 28.

54   John Calvin, *Institutes, Book II*, Ch. V., Section 5.

55   William Easum, *Dancing With Dinosaurs*, p. 61.

56   E. Stanley Ott, *The Vibrant Church*, p. 55.

57   Shawchuck and Heuser, *Leading the Congregation*, p. 185.

58   Gerald Renner, "Power Changes at the Mainstream's Helm," in *Progressions, A Lilly Endowment publication*, Vol. 2, Issue 1, January 1990, p. 11.

59   Malcolm Warford, "Denominational Seminaries Now," in *Christianity and Crisis*, April 8, 1991, vol. 51, p. 108.

60   James Fowler, *Becoming Adult, Becoming Christian* (San Francisco: Harper and Row, 1984), p. 7.

61   George G. Hunter III, *How to Reach Secular People*, p. 110.

62   Jacques Ellul, *The Presence of the Kingdom*, p. 3.

63   Eugene Peterson, *The Contemplative Pastor*, p. 96.

64   George G. Hunter III, *How to Reach Secular People*, p. 57.

65   Leander Keck, *The Church Confident* (Nashville: Abingdon Press, 1993), p. 19.

66   William Easum, *Dancing With Dinosaurs*, p.77.

67   Charles L. Rassieur, *The Problem Clergymen Don't Talk About* (Philadelphia: Westminster Press, 1976), pp. 17-42.

68   Leander Keck, *The Church Confident*, p. 65.

69   Linda-Marie Delloff, in *Progressions, Lilly Endowment Publication*, Vol. 2, Issue 1, January 1990, p. 13.

70   Jeanne Stevenson Moessner in Maxine Glaz and Jeanne Stevenson Moessner, "A New Pastoral Paradigm and Practice" in *Women in Travail and Transition: A New Pastoral Care* (Minneapolis: Fortress Press, 1991), p. 215.

71   Roger Heyns, Ph.D., President of the Hewlett Foundation, "Change, Church and the Seminary: Educating Today's Student for Openness to the Future," in *Theological Education for the Future*, Cincinnati, Foreword Movement Publications, 1988, p. 20.

72   Wilson Yates, "Seminaries: Back to the Future," *Christianity in Crisis*, April 8, 1991, vol. 51, p. 124.

73   George Barna, *Frog in the Kettle*, p. 53.

74   Henri Nouwen, *Creative Ministry* (New York: Doubleday Image Books, 1971), p. 6.

75   Ibid, p. 13.

76   Gerald Renner, "Power Changes at the Mainstream's Helm," in *Progressions*, January, 1990, vol. 2, p. 12.

77   Robert Don Hughes, "Future Seminary: A Science Fiction Story," in *Review and Expositor*, Volume 88, 1991, p. 208.

78   George Barna, *The Frog in the Kettle*, p. 180.

79   Tex Sample, *U.S. Lifestyles and Mainline Churches*, p.17.

80   Leander Keck, *The Church Confident*, pp. 47, 63.

81   Lesslie Newbigin, *The Gospel in a Pluralist Society*, p. 111.

82   *The Presbyterian Outloook*, April 4, 1994.

83   *The Presbyterian Outlook*, April 4, 1994.

84   Jean Caffey Lyles, "The Fading of Denominational Distinctiveness," in *Progressions, the Lilly Endowment*, January 1990, p. 17.

85   *The Presbyterian Outlook*, May 23, 1994, p. 3.

86   John C. Long, *Progressions, A Lilly Endowment Occasional Report*, "Presbyterians: A new look at an old church," January, 1990, p. 3.

87   Barbara Brown Zikmund, *Discovering the Church* (Philadelphia: Westminster Press, 1983), p. 89.